God Opens the Doors

GOD Opens the Doors

Bobbie J. Jobe

BROADMAN PRESS
Nashville, Tennessee

© Copyright 1987 • Broadman Press
All rights reserved
4250-41
ISBN: 0-8054-5041-6
Dewey Decimal Classification: B
Subject Headings: JOBE, BOBBIE J. // BLACK WOMEN—BIOGRAPHY
Library of Congress Catalog Card Number: 86-31005
Printed in the United States of America

Library of Congress Cataloging-in-Publication Data
Jobe, Bobbie J., 1939-
God opens the doors.

1. Jobe, Bobbie J., 1939-   . 2. Christian
biography—United States. 3. Afro-American nurses—
Biography. I. Title.
BR1725.J53A3 1987   286 [B]   86-31005
ISBN 0-8054-5041-6 (pbk.)

To my son Anthony,
one of God's precious servants,
and
to all those who need hope

Preface

"You can't do that!"

"Why can't I?"

"A black person has never been allowed to do it, that's why."

"Just watch me; I'll do it!"

The world is made up of many people, and their differences are astounding. Some see only hardships, while others welcome hardships as challenges. One says, "I can't"; another says, "I must."

I was fortunate enough to have parents who believed in the American dream. Neither poverty nor blackness had any lasting bearing on my future. Diligent effort would determine my station in life.

Many, many doors have been closed to me because of my skin color. Daddy said, "When one door is closed, look for the two other doors God has opened for you."

This book is an account of my following Daddy's instructions.

God Opens the Doors

1

January 12, 1939, at 1:10 AM, I became the nine-month-awaited blessing of Tom and Ruby Lee Ellis. Mom decided to name me Bobbie Jean.

She was only twenty when I was born. If I could describe her with one word, I'd say, "Alive." Her smile was infectious and quick. She stood 5 feet 5 inches tall and weighed 113 pounds.

Mom enjoyed playing dolls with me when I became a preschooler. No one could beat her sewing doll clothes or making paper doll clothes. Some days we baked. She became my best friend.

Dad was thirteen years older than Mom. Jokes and riddles came easily from him, and bedtime was my fun time with him.

My brother, Tom, Jr., was five years old when I was born. We didn't look alike or have the same interests. People claimed he looked like Mom and I looked like Dad.

As we grew, he enjoyed reading and playing his trumpet. I was always on the baseball, basketball, or volleyball team or running track.

We both were honor students. Tom, Jr.'s, grades

were high; he completely skipped the seventh grade. I had to study more than he did, but I enjoyed it.

We were also different in obedience. He required few spankings; I got into trouble daily. Trouble looked for me, it seemed.

"Bobbie, don't leave from here," Mom instructed.

Dusk was settling on a warm summer evening. Everyone gathered in our front yard. Bikes were ready for the nightly cruise. Tom, Jr., and his friends discussed the route while I played Russian roulette with "go or stay." *My brother will be there. What can happen to me?* I reasoned.

"Let's go," yelled Tom, Jr. About ten bikes took to the street. I followed.

We rode many blocks from our neighborhood. It was fun riding into the night. Mom insisted I needed a light on my bike before I could ride at night, but I wasn't having any trouble seeing. *Besides, it was no fun being left behind,* I thought as the cool breeze blew my hair.

Around nine each night we turned our bikes toward home. Sadness engulfed my independent spirit. Thoughts of Mom waiting to greet me brought tears to my eyes and a lump in my throat.

"What's wrong with you, Bobbie?" Tom, Jr., asked.

"Mama told me not to leave. I'm going to get a whipping when I get back."

"You do this every night. Why don't you stay home if you're afraid of getting whippings?"

Mom would be waiting as I expected. "Come on, young lady. Didn't I tell you not to leave from here?"

"Yes."

"Why did you disobey, Bobbie?"

"I just wanted to go too. Tom, Jr., was with me."

"I told you to stay here. You went anyway. So I'll have to do something I really don't like doing."

For years I got into trouble, but I always knew I was loved. Away from home I was often not loved.

A white kid taunted:

> "If you're white, you're all right;
> If you're brown, stick around;
> But if you're black, stay back!"

No one said, "I'm black, and I'm proud." To be born black meant trouble.

I was supposed to know "my place." Whoever decided my place had problems; they didn't know where they wanted to put me.

On the train, "my place" was up front. Blacks filled the first coach behind the baggage car. Being so close to the engine allowed smoke and embers to blow in on us through the open windows.

Noise pollution wasn't discussed, and air conditioning wasn't available, so windows had to remain open.

I had no place in the dining car. My food came from my grandmother's, Mama Daisy, lunch box. She prepared fried chicken, chips, boiled eggs, pickles, bread, various fruit, and cake or pie for us to eat en route.

Each summer I went with my grandparents to visit relatives in Houston. "Mama Daisy, when are we going to get there?" I questioned.

"We're getting closer," she answered.

"I'm tired, and it's so hot. Why does the train stop so much?"

"This is a mail train," Grandpa explained. "It's stopping to throw off mail and pick up passengers."

"Cold drinks; ice cream; candy; gum!"

"Get your cold drinks here. Anyone want a cold drink?" two black men asked.

They boarded the train and sold during one of the stops. My parched throat welcomed the cold soda.

"The situation was worse at one time," Grandpa commented. "You think being hot and a little dirty is bad. You should have rode the train a few years back."

"Why, Grandpa?"

"Why?—Because you would know what it's like to face a lynch mob."

"Who would they lynch?" I asked.

"Any colored person they saw. In some towns, colored people were told by the conductor to lower their window shades.

"What had the people done?"

"Nothing," Grandpa answered. "They were just colored."

On the bus, my place was behind the back door. When each of the seats was filled with a black person, other blacks stood. We couldn't sit in vacant seats in the white area.

In the hospital, my place was in the basement. When I was twelve, my tonsils were removed. Mom had two insurance policies, but it was the basement for me or nothing.

White and colored water fountains stood side by side. Both fountains were identical in appearance and in the liquid coming from them. I had to remember to drink from the colored water fountain.

Bathroom situations were different. White women and colored women didn't enter the same door. Neither did the doors stand side by side. The door marked "White Ladies" stood visible from almost any direction. To find the one marked "Colored Women" nearly required a map. After asking several people and being directed to the basement, I found my place in a faraway, dimly lit corner.

Paper towel and toilet tissue holders were usually empty. The heat and odor were unbearable. Sometimes I flew back outside as soon as I entered a colored bathroom.

"I'll wait until I get home," I said, or Mom asked, "Can't you wait until we go home?"

To most salespersons, my place was after every white received service. "First come, first served" didn't apply to blacks. Thank you and please were seldom used, either.

No downtown theater opened its door to me. My place to swim was in the only two pools for colored kids. And the zoo allowed me inside on my day, the nineteenth of June.

Everything was separate but not equal. We paid the required prices for inferior service.

"Mom, white people are funny, aren't they?"

"How do you mean, Bobbie?"

"I was thinking, They don't want us sitting by them or drinking from their fountain, but everyday colored women fill the bus going to care for their kids or cook for them."

"You're right." Mom's bright smile appeared as she half-whispered, "If all the cooks in America decided to poison their employers, we would kill about half of white America."

Those words were barely spoken when a knock sounded at the back door. Mom opened the door, and I saw a young, dirty white fellow standing outside.

"Miss, could you please give me something to eat?" he asked.

"Wait just a minute," Mom replied.

I smiled. She wouldn't poison anyone. Both of my parents were too busy feeding prodigal sons. Our house sat opposite a railroad track. Young, white hobos stopped daily to ask for help. We were a haven to many for years.

Mom returned shortly with a ham sandwich and a large glass of water. As he ate, we talked with him. He was trying to go home.

"I haven't been home in nearly five years. My mother is going to be surprised. I sure do appreciate this food."

Mom gave him some small change, probably enough to buy a cup of coffee and a sandwich. Then he was gone.

"Love thy neighbour" was a daily part of my childhood. I never saw anyone refused. Dad admonished, "If you can help a man, do it. God will repay you."

Black skin was not appreciated or valued by any race, I soon discovered. While attending segregated schools, I saw differences in the treatment of dark-skinned youth and fair-skinned ones or kids of professionals. Teachers allowed fair-skinned, straight-haired kids to run errands, erase the blackboard, or sit next to them at lunch.

"Daddy, they're not fair," I complained. "They let certain ones have leads in the play. And the same ones write names of people talking when the teacher leaves the room."

"Don't worry about that. Get something in your head, and nobody can take it from you," he would answer.

"But they're not fair."

"This world isn't fair, but there's always a way to get what you want. When a door is closed to you, look for the door God opens for you. Remember, the teachers have what you want. Learn all you can from them. You'll get your chance."

By the time I reached seventh grade, I knew the sting of rejection. Whether rejected by whites or blacks, the hurt was the same. I excelled scholastically, but I was beginning to withdraw into my own protected world when I met Mr. Henry Denson. He became my homeroom teacher and English teacher for three years. During that time, I observed him and learned to attempt any desired goal. Mr. Denson's quiet voice encouraged us.

"You can do it," he told us daily. When he said it, we believed him and tried.

Mr. Denson expected the best. He accepted nothing less. Work poorly done was returned and additional work assigned. We learned to strive for perfection. Unfair teachers were disliked by students not considered "cream of the crop." Everyone liked Mr. Denson because of his fairness.

"Bobbie, will you represent us on the decorating committee?" Mr. Denson inquired. I did exactly that.

I was proud of my achievements as a graduating ninth grader. I had dark skin and wasn't an offspring of professional parents, but I was recognized among the "chosen ones." Dad's instructions to put knowledge in my head were paying off.

The day of the junior prom arrived. Everyone talked about their escorts or their gowns. I could hardly wait.

Before going to school, I looked at my light green chiffon gown and three-inch-heel silver sandles. Without shoes I was five feet, seven and one-half inches tall.

"I'm glad Charles is tall," I told Mom.

The last period of the day I was excused from class. I went to the gym to help decorate it.

"Hi, Tommye," I said as I entered. "Where are the others?"

"Still in class," she answered.

"Why aren't they here?" I asked.

"They can't get excused."

"Well, why are they here?" I motioned to a group of fair-skinned kids.

"Their teachers let them out."

"They weren't selected to this committee."

"I know it," Tommye replied.

Something inside me snapped! *Too much of that positive thinker, Mr. Denson,* I guessed. I threw everything down and headed for the principal's office.

After stating the reason for my presence, I demanded that the other students be released. The principal looked flushed and helpless as he followed my demands.

That was my first time to stand up for what I believed to be right. I "bit the hand" holding my future, but it felt good.

In high school, I set goals and obtained them. I became president or vice-president of several clubs. Scholastically, I maintained my A average. For two school years I made straight As.

I became bold enough to try out for cheerleading. A singing voice I didn't have, but rhythm for motion I had. Each evening I practiced yells and dance motions. I loved "the old gold and blue."

"Mom, I know I'll be a good cheerleader if they choose me."

"You'll do all right."

"You don't understand, Mama. There are so many girls trying out."

"Do what you do every evening. You'll make it," Dad added.

The morning of tryouts, I walked to the center of the gym. My insides quivered. Practicing at home was one thing; performing before both PE instructors, Mrs. Belfrey and Miss Holloway, all present cheerleaders, and a gym half filled with spectators was another matter.

I planned to do a fight yell. With body in position and hands properly placed, I began:

"F-I-G-H-T—F-I-G-H-T—Fight team, fight! Fight team, fight—Fight! Fight! Fight!"

"Mama, I'm a cheerleader!" I yelled as soon as I reached home.

"What do we do now?" Mom asked.

"About what?"

"I know you'll need a costume."

"I'll tell you about that later."

My entire junior year was successful. Everyone knew me. My social life was a whirl of events that took second position only to grades.

When I was nine years old, I had started going to camp every summer. The summer before my senior year was no exception. A few things were different, though.

Instead of one camp, I was going to two camps. First, I would spend two weeks in an interracial camp. I would return to Fort Worth on a Saturday evening and would leave Sunday morning for Big Ben National Park with a group of Y-Teens from my school. Mom and I had planned both trips. Each night we had considered the clothes and equipment I needed. Everything had to be ready before I left because there would not be enough time to do anything between trips.

Having a mother so alive and caring was great. I was taller and heavier than she was, but my strides couldn't match her fast pace. Tom, Jr., and I were allowed to discuss anything we wanted. If Mom didn't know the answers to our questions, she bought books or checked them out of the library to obtain the facts. Since she was so young when we were born, we all grew up together.

Dad kept telling me to care about the abuses I saw. In tenth-grade English, I couldn't believe my ears.

One of the "cream of the crop" turned in an assignment without her name on the paper.

The teacher asked, "Whose paper is this? It has no name. I know you want credit for your work."

All heads lifted to be sure the paper wasn't theirs.

"It's mine. I thought I put my name on it," the student responded.

The teacher explained, "You better put your name on your papers. How will I know who I'm grading?"

Was she grading the written work or the writer? Differences between grades were less than a point for about ten students. Instead of giving me an A, I was cut back to an A- more than once. By shaving grades, the chosen ones could rank higher than we did.

Dad didn't believe in returning a hurt for a hurt. "Do unto others as you would have them do to you," he said. For nearly twelve years, I followed Dad's advice. But bitterness and resentment crept in. I didn't plan to remain quiet the way he advised.

One evening we began having problems on the bus. White students boarded first and occupied all the rear seats leaving us standing. When the bus reached our area, they stood and walked slowly to the front. This was a silent way of saying, "Now get in your place!"

The next day whites occupied rear seats again, so we took the first available front seats. Nothing was left to be occupied up front. Whites had to remain in the rear or stand. They were infuriated.

A few days later we discovered the battle wasn't

won. The bus arrived, and white students sat one to a seat. Books occupied the empty adjacent seats.

We weren't paying to stand, and they weren't paying for books to occupy a seat.

"Throw the books on the floor!" sounded throughout the bus.

Books were picked up as a white student challenged, "Don't touch my books!"

"I won't touch them if you move them," Jewel said.

"I'm not moving anything!" was the answer.

Books were slammed to the floor, on the laps of their owners, or out the bus window. We took our seats as the bus driver threatened to put us off the bus. He didn't instruct the white kids about their behavior.

The second week, white students sat two to a seat, up front. That's what they should have done at first.

Remembering those events disturbed me. *What will it be like to live two weeks with girls of other races?* I wanted to go to camp; I was sad too. Anyone can tire of fighting for her rights.

The day of departure arrived. Nothing could snuff out my anticipation.

"I'm going to enjoy myself," I vowed.

Mom and Dad stood with me in the Greyhound bus terminal.

"Where is Mrs. Robinson?" I asked.

"Settle down. She'll be here," Dad calmed me.

I needed my adviser. I was beginning to feel slightly shaky. *What will I do if she doesn't come?* I wondered.

"There she is!" I ran to meet her. Dorothy was with

her too. She was the only other black teenager going
from Fort Worth.

White girls seemed to be everywhere. Ten of them
had assembled by departure time. We exchanged
greetings and remained in our two groups.

At camp, Dorothy and I were assigned different
cabins. With heavy shoulders, I walked to my cabin.
Upon entering the cabin, I saw six white girls and one
black. The black girl was from the Galveston area.
She had lots of friends in camp. She joined them for
supper, and I met Dorothy.

I lay on my bunk that night quietly crying. *I want
to go home,* I thought. I had no friends around me.
I fell asleep crying.

About three days later, I stopped meeting Dorothy
for meals. She had new friends, and so did I. Girls of
my cabin began attending meetings and meals
together. Each night we talked about our boyfriends,
school activities, and music or dancing. We were
more alike than different. Racial matters were aired.
Whites expressed feelings I had had. They, too, had
not known what to expect. Some didn't know any
blacks personally. Jan's parents were rich and owned
a large ranch in West Texas. The only blacks she
knew worked on the ranch. She clung to me. I was
a totally new experience for her.

"Bobbie, we're going to have a candlelight service
tonight at the lake. Will you lead us in prayer? We're
trying to include as many girls as possible," an adviser requested.

"Yes, I'll do it."

The rest of the day my thoughts were, *What will*

*I say? I've never prayed aloud. These girls are of
different races and religions. What will be right for
all? I'm going to forget.*

That afternoon I prayed: "God, please tell me what
to pray. I want my prayer to mean something. It
must speak to each girl present. Please help me."

More than a hundred candles glowed in the summer night. Everyone not active in the program
waited on the south shore. Those participating in the
program waited on the north shore.

"We will have prayer by Bobbie Ellis."

My knees knocked, my hands were cold and wet,
and my mind screamed, *I'll mess up!*

As we walked back to our cabins from the lake,
individuals stopped me to talk. They said, "That was
a good prayer." "Your prayer meant a lot to me."
"Thanks for the prayer."

I knew God spoke and not me. I couldn't remember saying anything except "Heavenly Father."

No one slept that night. Daylight would bring our
departure. We exchanged addresses and signed auto-
graph books. We cried and promised to remain
friends.

While packing I thought, *I'll never see some of
these girls again. I'll never forget this experience.
Dad was right. For every bad white person, there are
two good ones. He had been trying to tell me: good
outnumbers bad. God, help me be a better person,
more like Dad."*

Sleep came as daylight dawned. Camp was hustle
and bustle in a few hours. We boarded camp buses
for our trip to the Greyhound and Trailways termi-

nals. Departure time varied for us. As different ones left, we clung and cried. Jan tightly hugged me as she cried, "Thanks for helping me understand."

Someone said, "Let's go get some soda."

Twelve of us piled into the snack bar and sat at the counter. We had gone to camp in two groups. Going home we were in one large group. Mrs. Robinson was responsible for all of us because the white adviser had remained in camp.

"We'll have a four-hour delay in Austin. Let's go sight-seeing."

"All right. Where can we go?"

Everyone made a suggestion, but all agreed to tour the capital.

"Niggers can't sit at my counter!"

An angry, young white male stared at me and Dorothy. He was ready to take the order if the two of us left.

While walking out, I repeated over and over, "This does not hurt. This does not hurt. Only sticks and stones can hurt. Talk doesn't hurt!"

I sat on the curb. Tears freely ran down my cheeks and dripped onto my chest. Words hurt badly. I couldn't lie to myself.

"Come on! Bobbie, I'll buy you a soft drink," one of my white companions consoled me. All had come to be with me.

"That's all right. I don't want one."

"Come on! You don't have to drink it, but we're buying it."

"That's all right," I repeated.

Hands pulled me to a standing position.

"Come on!" I was commanded.

I looked around and saw Dorothy sitting on the window ledge. She was fair skinned, so her grief was more visible than mine. Tears flowed down both cheeks, and her entire face was a bright red.

We stopped for her, then reentered. Again, the twelve of us sat at the counter. Blacks and whites had lived together in the woods for two weeks and together faced the fact that in cities, our black skin made Dorothy and me unacceptable to other whites.

The soda jerk returned. His face was as red as Dorothy's.

He mumbled, "I'm sorry."

Bullets can be removed; cuts and stab wounds can be repaired. How do you recall hateful words? The soft drinks arrived, and neither Dorothy nor I could even take the first sip. We received an apology, but the hurt remained.

In Austin, race relations were slightly better. We planned to eat before sight-seeing. Where to eat presented a problem. Service was available for the ten whites; no one downtown would serve the three blacks. I hadn't considered encountering prejudice in the capital of Texas.

"We're not going to eat if you can't," our companions said. The incident at the bus terminal had made the white girls determined to remain with us.

"Girls, your time is slipping away. What do you want to do?" Mrs. Robinson asked.

"We're going to find someone to feed us," our companions answered.

Mrs. Robinson continued, "You go ahead and eat.

I'll take Dorothy and Bobbie with me. As soon as we find a place to eat, we'll come back for you. Wait here for us."

We hailed a black taxi driver. He would know where we could eat.

"Do you want a dinner or just a sandwich?" he asked.

"I'm hungry; I want dinner," I answered.

"I know a place close to here. The food is good, and it's cheap too."

"Let's go!"

The food was delicious and inexpensive. While paying the cashier, we spied some good-looking pies.

"Let's take some back."

The girls had finished their meal and sat waiting for us.

"Oh, you have pie!"

"Yes, we brought enough for all of you."

"It is so good. I bet your meal was better than our sandwich," they said.

We only had time to tour the capital before the bus left for Fort Worth. We rode and relived the two weeks' experience. I would never forget those days.

I reached home and repacked for the Big Ben trip. Mama was happy to hear I enjoyed the interracial camp.

"I knew you wouldn't have any problems," she said.

At six the next morning, I waited outside the YWCA with twenty-five others. The Greyhound bus driver loaded our luggage, and we began our trip. We rode and rode. As dusk arrived, we began a climb into the mountains. I had no idea the trip would be so long. Having a bus needing repairs didn't help the situation, either.

We arrived, and cabin selection began. Six of us were in high school, so we begged to live together.

The area was beautiful. We climbed the mountains and attempted to enter the valley too. They said an Indian tribe lived there. We rode horses, did crafts, toured, and grew in the knowledge of outdoor survival.

Our day for washing dishes was approaching, so we began plotting. Instead of sleeping we discussed the situation.

"Our cabin is going to wash dishes Thursday."

"I'm not going to wash dishes."

"Every cabin has to do it."

"We don't."

"Why not?"

"We're old enough to do something else. Let's cook!"

"Yes, let's cook," everyone said.

We wrote the menu and listed all ingredients needed. We practiced selling the advisers our idea. Each girl decided the dish she would cook.

"All right girls, you can cook," Mrs. Daniels agreed.

Our day for action arrived. We began cooking the meal. Our idea was a little harder to do than to talk about. None of us had cooked such large amounts.

Shirley and I prepared peach cobbler for dessert. Everybody tasted every dish prepared.

"Oh! Oh! That's some good peach cobbler," we were told.

"We know it. Look at who cooked it," we replied.

"The stove is doing the cooking," another girl responded.

"You know what we mean," we said.

As the noon hour approached, we completed the meal.

"Shirley, come on. The cobbler's ready to take out of the oven."

"Take it out then."

"Are you crazy? I'm not going to lift this heavy pan alone. It's too hot."

We opened the door of the oven, and the pan looked even more enormous. We each had pot holders, but how could we reach inside to pick the pan up?

Shirley said, "Just catch one side and I'll get the other side." That sounded good. I had no suggestion any better. As we started lifting the pan, Shirley screamed.

"Oh! I burned myself!"

"Look at what you did!" I screamed seconds later. The pan had tilted, allowing hot cobbler to touch my hand. Naturally, I dropped my end. As we laughed, we watched cobbler ooze from the pan and form a pile on the floor.

"What do we do now? What can we use for dessert?" I asked.

Shirley said, "Hand me some bowls."

She scooped hot cobbler from the pile while saying, "This is good. It didn't touch the floor."

"We can't tell the others about this. You know they'll refuse to eat it," I said.

"I know," responded Shirley.

All of us agreed to conceal the facts about the dessert. When the meal ended, everyone complimented us. We laughed late into the night.

"Give me some more cobbler, please. I want some more cobbler," Shirley mocked the other campers.

"If they knew where the cobbler came from they wouldn't have touched it," I said.

Summer had been fun, but I anxiously waited for the first day of school. I was a senior with a completely new wardrobe. I felt as if I had the world on a string.

My entire senior year was fun. Extracurricular activities kept me busy. I was elected president of the Y-Teens and the Y-Teen Inter-Club Council; associate editor and news director of the *Terrellife* newspaper; president of the cheerleaders; vice-president of my homeroom; queen of the Y-Teen Mardi Gras; and a member of the volleyball and basketball teams.

How I found time to devote to so many things seems nearly impossible now. Mom wanted me to have fun, but not at the expense of lowered grades. I maintained an *A* average and graduated in the upper three percent of the class.

My efforts went unrewarded. Scholarships went only to those of the select group. I no longer felt any hurt. As the scholarships were announced, I believed there was a place in this world for me.

"I'll find my place," I whispered.

2

"Bobbie, I'm sorry, but we just don't have enough money to send you to college. We have to face facts. If you work, we'll be able to send you in January."

I heard Mom, but I didn't believe her. She thought there was no way; I believed God would provide the way. I had worked too hard to not get a chance to go to college. I had been selected as Senior Female Personality for the last issue of the *Terrellife*. The highlight of my life was to attend Los Angeles City College and major in psychology.

June and July passed without any discussion about college. I grew uneasy. *Am I going to have to stay home?* I wondered. *No, God will help me.*

"Would you like to go to Kansas City and visit your Uncle Henry for a while?" Mom asked.

Riding the train to Kansas City, Missouri, was very different from my rides to Houston. Sitting in the dome car allowed me to see in all directions for miles. The glass ceiling brought the outside in to the riders. I, also, had the privilege of eating in the dining car.

Everything seemed to have changed in a few years. I knew the change actually took many years to occur. Going to Houston, I had enjoyed eating from a lunch box. Going to Kansas City, I didn't consider carrying a lunch. It just wasn't done. Everyone would have considered the act uncouth.

Uncle Henry and Aunt Tempie made my visit happy. Most of the visit involved shopping. I was accumulating the clothes I needed for school. I still believed there was a solution to our lack of money.

After five days, I was ready to go home. College would begin soon. There were so many things I needed to complete. I would have to attend a local college since I had not made any other preparations. I didn't care; I just wanted to go anywhere.

September came, and Labor Day passed. My last friend went away to college. I was crushed. We really didn't have any money for college, and there were no available scholarships. For once, I wished I were one of "the chosen kids." Their parents had prepared for their future and getting all the scholarships helped too.

I cried and cried. Hurt and depression surrounded me. I couldn't think about January. Nothing happened in September, so why should I think things would be different in January. I was hurt because I couldn't change my situation. Mom was doing all she could; she had no cooperation, though. How do you express anger and resentment toward your father?

Daddy, with all his wisdom, had a flaw too. The defect wasn't apparent at all times. It popped up when least expected. I never considered the effect his life would have upon my future.

As a very young girl, even before kindergarten, I

remember going to Sunday School with Daddy. He was superintendent at the time. We attended one of the largest black churches in Fort Worth. I felt good inside when I saw Daddy studying the Bible. He attended local and state conferences and conventions. He was loved and respected.

When I entered fourth grade, I was aware of Daddy's problem. I couldn't accept the truth. Daddy had a drinking problem. *How could that be? Daddy loves God and attends church,* I reasoned.

Sometimes he wouldn't touch a drop of alcohol for months. During those times, life was fun and happiness. Hope surged through my body. *Maybe he really is through drinking,* I'd think. Then one Friday evening he wouldn't appear. Weekends and holidays were especially difficult for Daddy.

"Bobbie, take your fingers out of your mouth," Mom said. I obeyed. Daddy should have been home around 5:30. The clock said 6:30. *It's Friday. He's not coming. He's getting drunk.* I tried to still my thoughts.

Other thoughts began. *He's just late. He's not getting drunk. He hasn't had any alcohol in nine months. He enjoys church too much to slip back into bad habits. He doesn't go around those friends anymore. He's probably buying food for the picnic.*

"Bobbie, are you nervous? You're chewing your nails again," Mama reminded.

"No, I was thinking about what we're going to do on the Fourth of July. Are we still having our picnic?"

"Yes, if your Daddy comes home."

Mom voiced my fears. Failure was almost a certainty on any holiday. Dad would join his old friends to celebrate. He could not refuse that first drink. One drink sent him on a three- or-four-day binge.

"Please, God, don't let him drink," I prayed.

Drinking was the reason there was no money for college. The vicious cycle was about to begin again. Drink—pawn all valuables—gamble and lose entire paycheck—disappear for days—come home without one cent—use next check getting belongings out of pawn—struggle for months to pay delinquent bills— begin operating in the black—and back to drinking.

We didn't have the picnic, and we didn't go to the game. Daddy didn't come home for days.

Bang! Bang! Bang!

Only one person knocks like that. Daddy knocks like that when he's drunk. Fear raced through my body. Blood roared inside my head. Daddy's home. He's drunk too. I didn't need to see him or smell his breath. The knock told me why he was absent for three days.

"Hi, Jed," he bellowed at me.

Untidy and *disheveled* described the man standing before me. The tattered clothing on his body weren't his, and the worn, run-over shoes on his feet certainly weren't his.

I glared at him, as I eluded his hug. Everyone said I looked just like Daddy. I knew I was the "apple of his eye." At the moment, he was disgusting in my eyes.

"Get away." I pushed Daddy aside. "You're drunk again!"

"Did you see me drink anything?" he asked.

"I don't need to see you drink. I smell you."

"You don't smell anything! You're just guessing," he said.

"Your eyes are red as blood! And your breath will kill a dead man!" I responded.

Mom was ready to begin her interrogation. Dad's responses were just as silly and nonsensical as those made to me. He wanted to sleep; Mama wanted answers. I knew her frustration. We had hoped he wouldn't be intoxicated. We were disappointed again.

Ordinarily, Daddy was fun and extremely slow to anger. When he drank, his temper flashed like lightning during an electrical storm. I was always happy when he went to sleep. Chances of physical violence erupting were halted. When he didn't sleep, I feared imminent violence. As the fury of confrontation increased, so did the pounding inside my head.

"My head hurts, Mama."

"Where does it hurt, Baby?" Mama questioned.

"It's pounding here." I placed my hand to the area behind my right ear. "It feels like it wants to explode!" The pain became severe enough to cause me to cry.

Mom and Dad's disagreement ceased as they became a team working to stop my pain. I felt pain, but I have an idea I manifested the discomfort. It was my way to stop the confusion.

With all my former schoolmates away at college, Charles became the center of my life. We had been constant companions for three years. He graduated the year before I did and waited to go to college with me.

"I can't go this semester. You go. You have your basketball scholarship to use. Go ahead. It won't change the way we feel about each other," I said.

Charles, finally, followed my encouragement. I was lonely with him gone; I searched for a job in a white beauty salon. Cosmetology had been my main subject in high school.

I enjoyed giving facials, arching eyebrows, and giving manicures. Theory was no problem for me. Styling hair was not one of my strong points, so I planned to work in a white shop.

While reading the newspaper I saw something that caught my eye.

"Mama, here's an ad for a shampoo girl. It's a white shop. I think I'll call about the job."

Minutes later I said, "It's still available. I'm going for an interview tomorrow."

"Where is it?" Mom asked.

"At the Bluebonnet Circle. Do you know where that is located?"

"Not really. We'll get your father to take you."

The next day I secured my first job. As soon as I reached home, I called out, "Mama, I got the job."

"Good! Do you think you're going to like it?"

"Oh, yes. The Martins seem to be nice."

"Is it more than one?" Mama asked.

"It's a husband and wife team. They're both young and friendly. I think he's going to be rather quiet, but she's totally different. She's all over the shop in a flash."

"You like her, don't you?" Mama asked. Sometimes Mama knew me better than I knew myself. She knew I was happy.

"She's so happy. Her red hair is even 'happy,' " I said.

What would I have done if I had not followed Mama's advice to take a trade? Mama always was wise. There's no telling where she would have gone if she had received a college education.

Several months later, my life hit rock bottom. I was working, and my bank account was growing; I had ominous problems developing too.

Ring. Ring. Ring.

Mom called, "Charles is on the phone, Bobbie."

"Hi, Charles. I didn't know you were home."

"I came in this evening. Are you going to be home?" he asked.

"Yes, I'll be here. I have the answer," I said.

"What is it?"

"You'll have to wait until we see each other."

I hung up and cried again. Never had I been required to do something so difficult. Acting like an ostrich wouldn't help. The problem was going to become more apparent.

Charles arrived, and we went for a drive.

"What did the doctor say?" he asked.

"He said that I'm pregnant." Tears came again. *How could I tell Mama?*

"Bobbie, we'll marry," Charles reassured.

We had planned to marry. *Not like this*, I thought. *How could I have failed Mom so much?* If you play with fire, you may get burned. I couldn't change the situation. I didn't want to change it, but how could I tell Mama?

Several days later she asked, "Do you feel well, Bobbie?"

My heart sat in the center of my throat. "Yes, why?"

"You act different. You're quieter, and you're sleepy most of the time. You don't have a virus, do you?"

"I don't think so. Why?"

"You've had some nausea and vomiting." I had no idea Mama was aware of my symptoms.

"I'm madly in love," I bluffed.

"Something's wrong. You can't fool me."

She trained her eyes on me. I felt like a specimen under a microscope. Finally, Mom asked, "Are you pregnant?"

Just like that she said what I couldn't bring myself to say. I couldn't answer without lying.

"I'm not sure," I responded. The openness of our relationship was gone.

Again, Mom's searing eyes burned their way into my thoughts.

"You know if you are or aren't," she persisted.

Between laughs I blurted out, "I am." The floodgate to my tears opened. Attempting to laugh hadn't worked. We both cried. Mom said nothing else.

The next few days I realized my life was out of control. Charles talked about marriage but continued to attend college. Mom was cool and distant. I had never learned to share a problem with Dad.

"Oh, God, I wish I could die. I don't have anyone

to talk to. Please forgive me for this sin. Help me! Tell me what to do."

On my way home from the doctor, I casually browsed through downtown stores. I glanced at maternity clothes and baby clothes. Thoughts of getting married or the birth of my baby didn't bring me any happiness. I wanted things right between Mama and me. Our conversations were limited to monosyllables.

My eyes spotted an interesting item—a diary. "I can write my thoughts." My predicament was my fault. I didn't intend to worry anyone, but I needed to talk with someone.

That night I began my relationship with my silent friend. I wrote:

Dear Diary,

I'll share my joys and tears with you nightly. I don't want my children to make the same big mistake I made. What is the mistake? I became pregnant before I married.

I still love Charles and wish to have a normal, healthy, happy baby; be good parents; and provide a good, clean, and neat home.

Please, children, understand, and don't repeat our mistake. Go on and make us proud by finishing high school and college—then church weddings. Wishful thinking!!!

Dr. Stow became my doctor when my original doctor left town. Mama liked him and trusted his opinion. She was pleased that I selected him.

During my first visit with him, he asked, "Did you know you are Rh negative?"

"No, I didn't."

"Do you know what it means?"

"Not really. I think it has something to do with my blood."

Dr. Stow's discussion included the words *antibodies, positive, negative, blood exchanges,* and the importance of the condition to my unborn baby.

"You have nothing to worry about if your husband is negative, also. Have him come in for a blood test," he continued.

Charles had his blood tested the next day. He was positive.

Dr. Stow said, "Don't worry. I'll watch you closely. When you begin your sixth month, I'll have a blood test done every two weeks. It's a safety precaution. Usually, first babies aren't affected, though."

Dear Diary,

I am finally married! We have had a thousand laughs. First of all, we didn't get our license in Fort Worth because Charles told his correct age. He needed to be twenty-one. We loaded up the preacher and headed for Weatherford, Texas.

I held my breath when Charles said he was twenty-one. The preacher (justice of the peace) was a scream! He had the hiccups so bad we could hardly say our vows without laughing aloud. I wore something old, new, borrowed, and blue.

I'm happy and very much in love. I hope we find an apartment before the baby comes. God was with us. Today was the last day for our blood test. What if they had expired?

Dr. Stow calculated my delivery date for July 21. "I'm going to have a Fourth of July baby," I told everyone.

I opened my eyes the morning of the Fourth. Something woke me. *It's only 1 AM,* I thought.

"Oh! Oh!"

A terrible pain hit me in my lower back. I changed position as the pain hit again.

"Oh! Oh!"

Is it time to deliver? Surely not. Everyone said my stomach would drop and my water would break. I checked the position of my stomach. No change. I didn't know what I was looking for, but as long as things remained unchanged I considered everything all right.

Sleep wouldn't return. The annoying twitch in the bottom of my stomach wouldn't allow me to rest. I turned on my lamp and started reading.

At six I got up and prepared for a busy day. Just because I was pregnant, I refused to cut back on the work I normally did.

When Grandpa died, Mom had Mama Daisy's house enlarged and remodeled. We had moved in with her.

"Mama Daisy, get up. Shampoo your hair, and I'll do it for you," I said.

"Why so early?" she questioned.

"I have a lot to do before I go to the picnic."

The pains in the bottom of my stomach remained

unchanged. So did the position during the remainder of the day. I checked frequently for any changes. No one knew of my discomfort. When I finished ironing, I prepared potato salad and baked a cake.

Around 5 PM, I sat in the bathtub bathing when I realized the pains seemed harder and more frequent. Stomach position seemed unchanged, though. Charles and I were supposed to go to a picnic.

Everyone was at the dinner table. I called Mama to the bedroom.

"Mama, I'm having pains."

"For how long?" she asked.

"Since one o'clock this morning."

"And you're just now saying something."

"I wanted to be sure."

"How close are the pains?"

"They're coming every seven minutes."

"Don't eat anything. I'll call Dr. Stow."

I went into the kitchen to wait for instructions from my doctor. Everyone wanted to know if it were time.

"No," I said. I wasn't sure because I didn't know what to expect.

The smell of Daddy's barbecue ribs and beef tickled my nose. I knew Mama said don't eat; my stomach said eat. "I'm going to eat. I may not get to go to the picnic."

My pains became harder. When I felt one approaching, I ran and jumped into bed. As soon as I felt it leaving, I went back to the kitchen.

I placed a generous serving of ribs, beef, potato

salad, and baked beans on my plate. While I ate, Mama gave me my instructions.

"Dr. Stow said to continue timing your contractions and go to the hospital when the pains are five minutes apart," Mama said.

She threw in, "And stop eating!"

"Did he say that too?" I asked.

"No, he didn't, but he would if he knew."

Another hour passed before I decided it was time to go to the hospital. While Dad drove, I had time to think about the seriousness of the situation. Silently, I prayed.

"Father, I sinned, but I believe You have forgiven me. I ask You to stay by my side and help me through this birth. Please don't let anything happen to my baby. Let his blood be all right."

Mama said, "You're awful quiet. Have you stopped hurting?"

"No, the pain is still there."

"When you get to the hospital, don't try to stop hurting," she instructed.

I laughed until I cried.

"Mama, if I could stop these pains, I certainly would." As they joined me in laughing, the tenseness of the situation left.

At 8 PM we entered the emergency room.

"People are everywhere," I said to Mama. "Let's go home. It's a false alarm."

"You're here now. Go ahead and get checked."

I saw three pregnant women in the crowd. My pains had to be false labor. My stomach was much smaller than theirs, and their groans drowned out the slight sounds I made.

Mama whispered, "I haven't heard you make a sound. Are you too afraid to hurt?"

She was right. I hadn't felt one pain since we arrived. Fear gripped me. I looked at her and joined her in laughing.

I said, "I'm not hurting anymore. These people are hurting for me."

"Mrs. Miller, I'll check you now," a nurse said. She returned a few minutes after finishing the exam.

"Dr. Stow called in some orders for you. He's on his way."

"Do you mean, I'm not going home?"

"No, you're being admitted."

"It's not false labor?" I asked.

"No, we should have a baby before breakfast," she replied.

The doctor's orders, including an injection, were followed in preparing me for delivery.

"Are you all right, Mrs. Miller?"

"Yes, I'm all right but a little nauseated. I'm going to vomit." I vomited and vomited. I thought I would never stop. Mama had been right. I should not have eaten. Instead of the injection bringing rest, it brought the agony of vomiting. I prayed my entire delivery wouldn't be as confusing.

I dozed between pains. They had to be pretty severe. Each one caused me to sit straight up in bed and moan loud and long. Perspiration covered my body.

I opened my eyes and realized my parents were gone. Charles sat by my side.

"Oh! Oh! Oh! I moaned loudly. A gigantic pain threatened to rip my back asunder. I attempted a hasty exit over the back of the bed.

Charles commanded, "Lay down, Bobbie." I obeyed, until the next wave of pains approached.

Later, I opened my eyes and wondered aloud, *How did I get here?* I was in another room. I looked about. It looked like an operating room, and everyone was dressed in surgery clothes.

"You're in the delivery room," a nurse answered. "You'll have your baby very soon. Everything is all right." She was experienced enough to recognize my unspoken fear.

"Oh! Oh!" I arched my back.

"Bobbie, how are you feeling?" It was the clear, friendly voice of Dr. Stow. I looked over my head and recognized his face behind a mask. Knowing he was with me brought me comfort. I could relax. He knew what to do.

Labor pains continued to increase in strength and frequency.

I heard Dr. Stow again, "Bobbie, strain down for me." I obeyed until a pain feeling like fatality cut through my back.

"Bobbie, you're about to have your baby. I'm going to give you some gas. Just breathe it in," Dr. Stow instructed.

When I had my tonsils removed, I had fought the ether. During the delivery, I gulped the gas. The odor wasn't pleasant, but I was ready to accept anything that would free me of my pains.

"Bobbie," someone called.

I opened my eyes. Now I was in my hospital room. Dr. Stow stood by my bedside. He had called my name.

"You have a healthy little boy, Bobbie. Everything went fine. He didn't need a blood exchange. He's fine. You can see him a little later." Dr. Stow said.

I was sleepy, but not too sleepy to be hurt. I planned to have a girl. I never entertained the thought of birthing a son. I couldn't name him Angela. It was night before I was awake enough to see my son. He arrived covered in a blue blanket. The nurse proudly handed him to me and watched my expression.

I exposed him entirely. I counted his fingers and toes twice. He looked at me from one open eye.

"He's so small," I said.

"He's a big baby, six pounds, ten and one-half ounces," said the nurse.

"Are you sure he's mine? He's so red."

The nurse laughed. "He's yours. His color will darken when he gets into the sunlight."

"His hair is so pretty," I said. Tiny black curls covered his entire head. How could people say there is no God? What could produce a complete human from a seed smaller than a dot?

"Look at his eyebrows. God painted them perfectly, didn't He?" I said.

"That He did," the nurse responded.

"Why are his legs like this?" They were flexed upon themselves. "He's curled into a circle."

"He's been in that position nine months. He'll unbend in a few weeks. Let him discover he has room to move about," the nurse answered.

Blacks weren't admitted to the basement of the hospital any longer. We occupied a ward. I had five roommates. My baby was smallest and the only male. While the girls slept, he nursed.

The other mothers said, "He's a good eater. You're not going to have trouble out of him."

When Anthony Eugene Miller was three days old, he was circumcised. The next day I went home with my bundle of joy.

Mama had adopted Tom, Jr.'s, daughter when she was six months old. Jean waited anxiously for me to put Anthony down.

"Bobbie, let me hold him! I want him! Let me hold him!" she begged.

"All right. Sit down."

She ran and sat in her little red rocker and opened her arms.

I thought, *She should have been mine.* I couldn't love Anthony anymore than I loved her. She was such a pretty child. Mama thought I spoiled her. When she started to kindergarten, I bought her a dress for every day of the month. She didn't have to wear any dress twice in the same month.

I stooped down and placed Anthony in her arms. As I straightened up, I caught a glimpse of my figure.

"Look, Mama Daisy, no more stomach." I wore a straight, form-fitting skirt. I had been the only mother in the ward who didn't have a large stomach after delivery.

"Do you like him, Jean?"

"Can I keep him? I want to play with him," she answered.

"He's not ready to play yet." I could see she loved him as I loved her.

A week later, my bundle of joy became a bundle of woe. Tears streamed down my face.

"What's wrong, Bobbie?" Mama asked.

My tears flowed harder.

"I'm tired of this baby."

"Well, you can't give him back. What's the matter?"

"He wants me to hold him. I'm sleepy."

"It's only 2 AM," Mama said. She smiled and hugged me. "He has his days and nights confused. He'll change. He can't sleep all day and night, too."

"I need to be sleeping. I've got to be on the bus stop by 6 AM."

"I know," Mama said.

I loved my son, but I had no plans to increase my brood. While I learned the responsibilities of motherhood, Charles had his hands filled with a basketball.

Dear Diary,

I'm not sure about this marriage. I want a happy home. I can't be father and mother to Anthony. I promised God I would give the baby the best I had to offer. I refuse to "shortchange" him. I'll try a little longer.

Mama was wise. She helped me, but the bulk of Anthony's care was my responsibility.

She said, "You need to learn what it means to be a mother. You will not be wanting another baby soon."

Charles's irregular attempts to assist with Anthony's care or financial needs hurt deeply. I was younger than he. If I could assume my responsibilities, why couldn't he?

Mama was right again.

She said, "He's a nice fellow. He's too immature, though." She didn't attempt to pressure me into thinking as she did.

I worked three days a week, Thursday through Saturday, at another white beauty shop. Rae was as good an employer to work for as the Martins had been. I wanted more out of life than shampooing someone's hair, though.

For weeks I considered my future. Did I have a future? If I went to school, what could I complete without taking years to do it?

Dear Diary,

Today is my first Mother's Day. Being a mother is a big responsibility. I thank God for my son. Where do I go from here? I can't continue in this farce of a marriage. I believe life should be happier. Please, God, show me the way.

I guess my new decision showed on my face. A few evenings later, Mama asked, "Bobbie, have you thought about your future? What do you plan to do with your life?"

"I want to go to school."

"What kind of school?" she questioned.

"Nursing school. I'm trying to decide whether to be a registered nurse or a vocational nurse."

"Remember our saying, 'Reach for the stars, but climb one day at a time.' Where do we begin?" she asked.

I always thought I had the best mother. She forgave me and was ready to help develop any dreams I had. "God, help me be this kind of mother to my son."

3

"Mama, I'll be late tonight. I'm going to stop by the library again."

"What are you doing in the library every evening?" Daddy asked.

"I'm trying to learn as much as I can about nursing. There's so much to decide."

"Like what?" Daddy continued.

"Like which school should I consider. There are thousands of them."

"Do you mean locally, in the state, or out of state?" Mama asked.

"I'm trying to find one in the state that will accept me. Only a few admit blacks."

I selected three and wrote them that night. A month passed without any reply.

"Mama, I guess they're not going to answer. Maybe I wasn't supposed to be a psychiatric nurse."

"What's a psychiatric nurse?" Jean asked.

My little niece was growing into an attractive young girl. Her love of Anthony had deepened. He was her living doll.

I answered, "A psychiatric nurse cares for people with mental problems."

"We need a psychiatric nurse to tell us what's wrong with your father," Mama quipped sarcastically.

Daddy had just returned from a drinking bout. I did not understand Mama. If she didn't like Dad's drinking, why wouldn't she leave him?

The next day I received an answer from a nursing school in Dallas, Texas.

"What did they say?" Mama asked. Her eyes jumped around in excitement.

"I'm trying to find out now." I finished reading before answering again. "I need to go to Dallas on the fifteenth of this month to take my pre-entrance exam."

I rose at dawn the morning of the fifteenth. I was anxious to begin my new life. I wasn't divorced, but I had closed the door on the life I once had with Charles. The experience was costly and valuable.

Daddy drove me to Dallas for the test. At 9 AM I entered the testing area. Girls were everywhere. *Why are we all blacks?* I wondered. The school was more than 95 percent white. Why so many blacks?

The examination was given in two major sections. At the conclusion of the first half, we eagerly talked of our aspirations.

"Mrs. Miller, could we speak with you a moment?"

"Yes," I answered.

As I followed the nurse I thought, *Have I failed?* I entered an office and was invited to sit. Another nurse entered, and the two began talking.

"Mrs. Miller, we briefly checked your test results and you scored high enough to go on with the second half. We would like to ask you a few questions."

I nodded in agreement. They could ask anything. Knowing I hadn't failed felt good.

The two began firing questions in my direction.

"How will you pay for your schooling?" "Can you afford to pay for the entire course?" "How does your husband feel about you going to school?" "Will you have time to study?" "Who will keep your baby?" "If your baby should get sick, will you have to drop out of school?"

I answered each question as soon as it was asked. I maintained eye contact with both nurses while answering. Confidence flowed through each answer.

"Mrs. Miller, we like your answers. You can go ahead with the second half."

We returned to the testing area. My test companions were told they had not scored too highly. The second half of testing involved a fee. Anyone wanting to continue could. Maybe they would raise their low scores, but going on was not encouraged.

About ten of us began the second half, as the rest left. I knew why we were all black. The school wanted a few "tokens" for the new class. One or two blacks among fifty or seventy-five whites was supposed to reveal integration.

A few weeks later, I received instructions for enrolling.

"I'm accepted!" I squealed. Mama and I danced around the kitchen. Our conversation trailed off into plans for my departure.

Dear Diary,

I was accepted in school today. I should be happy, but I'm not. I didn't know what was wrong until after I prayed. I don't want to be a token. I have to think of Anthony. My marriage is over, but he needs a father. I don't believe a school with so few black girls will have very many black men around. I pray Mama will understand.

Saint Joseph Hospital in Fort Worth had a professional nursing school. If I went there I could stay home. I wrote and stated my interest in becoming a registered nurse. A few weeks later I received instructions for admission. I was to take a preentrance exam as I did in Dallas.

Test morning I dressed and rode the bus to the hospital. I entered the test area and saw one black face in a sea of white faces. I nearly laughed aloud. From all black to nearly all white: more tokens.

The girls were friendly and talked freely with me. I relaxed and forgot skin color.

"Girls, do you have any questions?" No one said anything. The instructor continued. "Work rapidly. Don't spend too much time on one question. You can always come back to those you aren't sure about. Open your test booklet. Read the instructions. Begin."

I followed the instructions involving my name and other vital data. Then I started reading the questions.

Oh, God, I can't think! I prayed as I reread question six. I still couldn't think. *Please, God, help me remember.*

Everything remained a blank. I read questions 7, 8, 9, and 10. I couldn't remember, nor reason. *I'm failing!*

"Stop please," the instructor instructed after an hour.

I stopped. Hurt doesn't describe the intense pain inside my chest. I had answered about ten questions. During the remainder of the exam, my performance remained unchanged. I continued to pray, but my brain was out to lunch, a four-hour lunch break. At times tears fell silently from my eyes. *Jesus, I'm failing,* I prayed as I cried.

I cried most of the way home. I needed Mama's reassuring voice and touch. One look at my face, and Mama knew; I was totally distressed.

"It didn't go too well, did it?" she asked.

I didn't answer; I couldn't speak. I cried, nearly as long as I did when I told her of my pregnancy. When I did speak, I spoke with determination.

"Mama, I'm going to pass my next test."

I wrote a number of schools and received either no answer or a rejection. Pickings within the state became nearly nonexistent. Blacks weren't accepted with open arms.

With a heavy heart, I wrote to a school in Los Angeles. I wanted to become a nurse, but I didn't want to be very far from Anthony. Mama planned to keep him; I didn't want him to forget me.

While walking downtown one evening, I saw Dorothy Jackson. Our contact had been limited since we returned from the interracial camp.

"Hi, Bobbie."

"Hi, Dorothy. Where have you been?"

"I'm attending Lincoln University," she said.

"That's in Missouri, isn't it?"

"Yes, Jefferson City."

"Do you like it?"

"I love it. What have you been doing?" she asked.

"I'm trying to get into a nursing school."

"Bobbie, there's one of the best nursing schools in the country in Saint Louis."

"Well, tell me about it."

"It's mostly run by blacks. They say it's one of the largest black hospitals in the world. And their nurses have good reputations."

"How long will I have to attend?"

"Three years, I think," Dorothy replied. "I'd try it if I were you."

I smiled while asking, "How's the male situation?"

"Unending! You'll be surrounded by military bases, colleges, and I don't know how many hospitals."

"Do you know the address?"

"No, I don't. Just write to Homer G. Phillips School of Nursing, Saint Louis, Missouri. They'll get it."

"I'll do it tonight."

While walking to the bus stop, I saw Samuel Hill. He was attending the same college Dorothy attended. I had not seen him since we graduated. We talked a while. He was as positive about Homer G. Phillips as Dorothy had been.

A letter arrived from the nursing school in Los Angeles. My credentials had been accepted. I was instructed to go to Southern Methodist University for the National League of Nursing preentrance examination.

The word *national* made me feel uneasy. I recalled my performance at Saint Joseph.

"What do you plan to do?" Mama asked.

"I'm not sure. I failed so badly last time."

"Did they give you those *As* in high school?"

"Getting those grades was like pulling teeth, teeth not loose!"

"I believe you can do it," Mama continued.

I browsed through a catalog later that night. The pages flipped from the clothing section to the book section. As I reached to turn to the clothes again, my eyes saw *How to Prepare for College Entrance Exams.* I began to read about the book. It, apparently, was a detailed manual of various types of tests. I could study and practice in my weak areas while waiting for the next test date. The next day I bought the book. That night I began my self-training.

"This is my last attempt. I'll sink or swim," I told Mom.

I rode the bus to Dallas to SMU for another test. I believed I was going to pass. Neither fear nor anxiety accompanied me. I entered the test area and received a shock. People were everywhere! Whites, blacks, young, old, males, and females sat throughout a large auditorium. We talked while waiting to begin the first test.

The NLN examination was required by hundreds of schools. Our grades would be sent to any schools of our choice.

I had heard from Saint Louis, and that school required the same preentrance test that the Los Angeles school required. My grades were to be sent to both schools. "I'm going to put my eggs in more than one basket," I had told Mama. If I didn't gain entrance to one, maybe I would be accepted in the other one.

We received instructions similar to those given at Saint Joseph. Then the familiar phrase "You may begin" was spoken.

I worked rapidly and confidently. My brain was not on a lunch break. I thanked God for that. This was the hardest test of the three. It required an entire day to complete.

At lunch I met several other black girls who planned to go to Homer G. too. Some complained of not understanding various math sections on the exam. I told them about the book I had used.

As soon as I reached home I called out, "I passed! I passed!"

"How do you know?" Mama questioned. "Did they grade the test?"

"No, not yet"

"How do you know you passed?"

"I know I did. The questions were too easy."

"What do we do now?" Mama asked.

"Wait to see which school accepts me," I replied.

I couldn't wait. I began shopping for clothes within a week.

About two weeks passed before I heard anything official. The school in Los Angeles contacted me and welcomed me to its nursing program. Two days later I received a letter from Homer G. I had been accepted by both schools. Decision time: I couldn't attend both schools. I decided on Homer G. because it was closest and I could come home twice a year to see Anthony.

"Sure are a lot of forms here," I said as I looked through papers from Homer G.

"What are they?" Daddy asked.

"Information blanks. There is a form for a physical, one for a dentist, and one for an opthalmologist."

"What's that?" Mama asked.

"I don't know," I said. "Let's see what it is." I located the word in my dictionary and began reading, "A doctor who specializes in ophthalmology."

"That doesn't tell me much," Mama said.

"I'll read the definition of *ophthalmology.* 'The branch of medicine dealing with the structure, function, and diseases of the eye.' "

"Why didn't they say eye specialist?" Mama asked.

I responded, "They did. You wanted a ten-cent word. They used a fifty-cent word." We both laughed.

Dr. Stow completed my forms after doing my physical. He and his nurse spoke encouragingly. I promised to visit when I came home.

My dental forms were completed after one extraction and one filling.

"Two down and one to go," I said to Mom. "I'll make an appointment tomorrow for the eye exam."

I selected a doctor from the Yellow Pages and dialed the number.

"I'm sorry, but our doctor doesn't see colored people." I hung up in disbelief.

"What did she say?"

"She said her doctor doesn't see colored people."

"Call another one," Daddy said.

He was the same old father. He didn't waste words on the receptionist's statement. He remained positive.

I called not one other but two others. Each informed me that colored people weren't served.

"Call another one," Mama said. "We'll call every eye doctor in the directory! Don't give up. You've come too far now."

"You're right. I didn't get my tooth pulled for nothing!" I said.

We laughed; I was serious. Dentists weren't my favorite people. The one who pulled my tooth was a "horse doctor." He nearly "killed" me. It was partly my fault for not seeking aid sooner.

Call number four brought positive results. I received a 9 AM appointment for the next day.

I dressed early and waited for Mama to get ready. I tasted the sweetness of success. This was the last preentrance requirement I needed to complete.

We entered the doctor's office, and a receptionist gazed steadily at me as she said, with no hint of any emotions, "Our doctors don't see colored people."

As we left, Mama said, "There's another one in this building. Let's see if we can get an appointment."

We rode the elevator down to the second floor, located the office, and entered. We were about to inquire when a red-faced, stammering receptionist said, "I'm sorry. Our doctor doesn't see colored people."

I waited outside for Mama to join me. My head pounded. And I wanted to pound someone.

"Bobbie, she said a doctor in the Medical Arts Building might do the examination."

"Forget it! I'm not going across town to get another rejection."

"What about your tooth?" Mama teased.

"Let's go," I said.

As we rode, I mocked, "I'm sorry. Our doctor doesn't see colored people."

Mama said, "I thought you said those doctors were eye specialists."

"I did."

"Well, why do they keep saying, 'Our doctor doesn't see colored people'? We want the doctor to see your eyes."

Mama always was fun. I couldn't have requested a mother any better.

We located the proper office and heard the familiar rejection. I walked out with my head held high. Mama always said, "No one can make you feel inferior unless you allow it." I felt great. I had given it a good try. Maybe the school would allow me to enter without the eye test being done. Maybe I could have it done easier in Saint Louis. I hadn't given up. It was time to try another alternative.

Again Mama joined me late. "Bobbie, there's another one upstairs."

We both smiled and said together, "Remember the tooth!"

We located the office. Inside, white people sat everywhere. We told the receptionist of our need.

She said, "Wait in here," as she led us to an office in the back. "I'll see if the doctor will see you. We don't, generally, see colored people." She closed the door behind her when she left.

"Don't let anyone see the two apes in the back room," I clowned with Mama.

She said, "Don't knock it. We are sitting."

"But for how long?" I asked.

The receptionist returned and said, "He'll see you. Wait in here." She closed the door and left.

"Mama, I bet an orangutan wouldn't have as much trouble getting his eyes examined as we have had."

"Don't you realize you are a Negro?" she answered.

I read and dozed. Finally, the door opened.

"The doctor will see you now."

We exited to an empty waiting room. We were the last to be seen. I had been right. No one was supposed to see us.

The doctor was friendly and seemed genuinely interested in my goals. He talked freely with me while having me read the eye chart, look in various directions, relate when objects came into focus or disappeared, and state colors seen.

He completed my form, then extended his hand for a farewell shake.

"Come again, Bobbie, if I can ever help you. There's no charge."

I quit my job at Vernon's Beauty Salon two weeks before school was to begin. Mama said I needed a rest. I was too excited to rest. She gave me three new, one-hundred dollar bills to add to the money I had saved. I would have accepted three old, one-hundred dollar bills. All of the money was for clothes and shoes.

Departure day came, and I hurried through the day. Dad carried my luggage to the train station. I spent most of the day with Anthony.

He questioned, "Mommie, where're you going? I want to go. Why can't I go?" His language was excellent for a thirteen-month old. He couldn't understand why he could not go too.

Mama said, "Bobbie, we better go. Your train will be in soon." Doubts came flooding in on me.

"Am I doing the right thing? What if I can't be away from my son for three months?"

I looked at my chubby, chocolate son. Anthony's eyes were two round, glistening black balls. Two deep dimples appeared with each smile. He was a happy and obedient child.

I'm doing the right thing. He'll be all right with Mama, I reassured myself.

4

At 9 AM the next day, I arrived in Saint Louis. Suddenly, I realized what I had done. I was alone in a strange city. I knew no one! People rushed all around me. No one spoke as people did in Texas. I was going to have to think for myself.

"What do I do, Lord?"

I went to the baggage room and collected my luggage. I waited with others. My wardrobe trunk hadn't come to the baggage room yet.

"Taxi! Taxi! Anyone want a taxi," a man yelled.

"I need a cab," I answered.

"Is this all of your luggage?"

"No, I have a trunk too."

"Go ahead and get it. I'll wait for you."

The baggage man brought my trunk forward, and I gave him my claim ticket.

"Where do you want me to put it?" he asked.

I looked at the taxi driver, and he said, "Lady, that trunk won't fit in any cab. Do you have someone to pick it up for you?"

"No, I don't know anyone in Saint Louis."

The taxi man removed his cap and scratched his

head before speaking again. "Here, give me your claim ticket. I'll bring the trunk to you when I get off." I handed him the ticket; he picked up my two suitcases, and we were off.

Saint Louis looked nothing like Fort Worth. All the houses were like buildings. They were two or more stories tall. I didn't see grass and flowers in yards. It was unbelievably hot. I needed no one to tell me the humidity soared.

A young and cheery female, a junior student, greeted me at the dormitory door. She took my luggage and escorted me to my room. Girls, friendly girls, called out to me as we walked.

I repeated, "My name is Bobbie Miller. I'm from Fort Worth, Texas," at least ten times before reaching the fifth floor.

I entered my room and saw a girl sleeping on one of the beds.

"Hi, I'm Bobbie Miller. I'm from Fort Worth, Texas," I cheerfully said.

The sleeping girl raised her head, half opened her eyes, yawned, and said, "Hi, I'm Grace Adams. I'm from Saint Louis." Her head went back down on the pillow; her eyes closed, and she returned to sleep.

"How could she sleep the first day of school?" I unpacked my two suitcases and joined my classmates in greeting others. We were from countless states and cities, girls of all descriptions, and graduates in the upper 3 percent of our high school classes.

After supper I began to worry. The taxi man had not come. When 6:30 arrived, I went to Grace.

"Grace, my trunk hasn't come, yet."

"How is it supposed to come?" she asked.

"The taxi man is bringing it. I gave him my claim ticket."

"What's his name?"

"I don't know."

"Who does he drive for?"

"I don't remember."

Grace's eyes grew large. "What did he look like?"

My eyes were becoming watery. "He was a young, white man," I replied.

"Girl! Do you mean you gave your claim ticket to an unknown white man?"

"Yes, he told me he would bring the trunk when he got off."

"You must be crazy! You don't give anybody your claim ticket. You can't describe the man, you don't know his name, and you don't know who he drives for. Forget those clothes. They're gone!" A dimpled smile appeared, and she suppressed it.

Tears started down my face. All my new clothes were inside the trunk.

"What will I wear?" I couldn't remain in school without those clothes. Mama wouldn't be able to replace them. I went to our room and lay, crying on the bed.

Grace came in and said, "I'll call my father, but I don't know what he can do."

RING! RING!

We looked at each other. The sound was new to us. Then we realized it was the buzzer we had been told about. A ringing buzzer meant one of us had a visitor. We went downstairs together.

The elevator door opened, and in the center of the lobby sat my trunk. I looked at Grace with a look of triumph.

"I knew you would come," I said to the cab man. I really said that for Grace's benefit. People weren't any different in Saint Louis than those in Texas. Nice people live everywhere.

Riding back up to our room, Grace cautioned, "You're lucky this time. I hope you never do anything that stupid again. You may not be as lucky next time."

Classes didn't begin at once. The week began with touring the hospital. I had no idea Homer G. Phillips was so large. The hospital was shaped like a double *Y* and consisted of five floors, a basement, and a sub-basement. A long winding tunnel connected the hospital to the nurse's dorm. There would be no need to go outside to reach the hospital during inclement weather.

"This hospital has everything," I wrote Mom. It did too. There was a school for radiology students, laboratory students, professional nurses, practical nurses, and training for social workers, interns, chaplains, diet therapists, and dentists.

My letter was several pages long. There was so much to tell:

Mama, the hospital is run mostly by blacks! This huge place runs smoothly by black people. The administrator, director of nursing, director of education, all my instructors—just everybody is black!

Now get ready for this: The hospital staff looks like

a United Nations assembly. I think every race or nationality in the world is here. When they come to meals in their native dress, it's a beautiful sight.

I wasn't able to decide about the staff we met during our tour. Most seemed friendly and professional. Others spoke, but I felt no sincerity coming from them. Our presence was being tolerated, not welcomed. Everyone wanted to know when we would start working.

"They don't work. They come to the wards for clinical experience," Miss Whiteside, a clinical instructor, reminded them.

For five days we toured different scenic sites. The public zoo impressed me most. The prospect of professional baseball and football thrilled me. I could hear cheers from Bush Stadium in my room. Daddy would have enjoyed attending the games.

The second week began, and I realized playtime was over. The instructors didn't discriminate or pamper any of us. We determined our own future. They would assist in any way possible, though.

I had made *As* during my twelve years of school. When informed of their grading scale, I expected few As. Their system was:

A	92-100	Superior
B	93-91	Good
C	74-82	Average
D	65-73	Unsatisfactory
F	Below 65	Failing

My spirits plunged when told the results of my preentrance exam. I had felt so confident after the test. God had to have guided them in their decision to accept me. I ranked about twenty-eighth in a class of thirty-four.

What am I doing here? I should have stayed home with my son. I wanted to go home. I couldn't wait to escape my final class after being given such discouraging news.

"Hello, Mama," I said after she accepted my collect call.

"Hi, Bobbie. How are things going for you?"

"Mama, I want to come home." The tears were flowing by then. I wasn't able to pretend everything was fine.

"What's wrong, Baby?" Mama calmly asked.

"I just want to come home," I said.

"Bobbie, I know you miss us and Anthony, but do something for Mama, will you?"

"What?"

"Give it another try. This is just your second week. You're beginning to miss us. It'll get better. Will you try?"

"All right, Mama."

Then we talked about every new feat Anthony was accomplishing until Daddy said, "Have you two forgotten you are talking long distance?"

Miss Doris Mosley was responsible for getting us operating in the right frame of mind. She was professional but tough. Her "bark" was loud and rough, so I hoped her "bite" wasn't as severe.

"You little people can just decide now whether you want to be nurses or not. We have no time to play with you. Nursing has no place for immaturity. Your actions involve life and death every day. If you can't shape up, we will ship you out," she informed us. Coming late to her class or sleeping during lectures wasn't tolerated. She assisted with improving our personal appearance. While restyling our hair and teaching us about walking, standing, sitting, and lifting, she was as much fun as Mama.

The third week my spirits began digging a hole in the dirt. I hadn't thought I could feel worse than I did the second week. In high school I successfully completed geometry, physics, biology, and trigonometry but never tackled chemistry. We were to complete organic and inorganic chemistry in three months. For most students, it would be a review.

I struggled to understand formulas and symbols. Attempting to solve equations was totally unsuccessful. I had positive and negative as confused as when Anthony got his days and nights turned around.

Friday evening I dialed Mama again. It had been another week.

"Hi, Mama."

"Hi, Bobbie. How are things?"

"Mama, I want to come home. I don't think I can make it. I don't understand anything going on."

"Bobbie, did they give you those As in high school?"

"No."

"Well, you must have the ability to learn. You haven't given yourself enough time. Will you try one more week for me?"

"I guess so."

"Good! I have someone wanting to talk to you."

"Hello, Mommie. When you coming home? You going come get me?"

I answered each of Anthony's questions. He had received the red car coat I bought the first weekend I went shopping. Mama said it fit perfectly.

That night while Grace slept, I slipped to my knees. "Heavenly Father, I need Your help. I have too many people making sacrifices for me. I can't fail them. Please help me learn the things I must know." I remained on my knees as the tears started. I wanted my baby. How could I stay away from him for three months? I had no other choice, if I wanted to make my parents proud of me.

From the unknown, an idea formed. I would pray and ask for God's assistance each time I bowed my head at meals and at bedtime. I seldom missed meals, so I would be praying at least four times every day.

At breakfast I began my routine of talking with God. My confidence peeped from the hole it had dug. Making beds that morning was an easier task.

Mama taught me to clean my room, wash the dishes, and make the beds each morning before going to school. My room looked neat; the bed was tidy.

Hospital beds had a whole new set of rules and goals. Neatness wasn't the only concern. I was learning the importance of economy of time, effort, material, and neatness of finish.

Sheets were never to touch the floor—not even dirty ones. I was not to walk around the bed while making it. I completed one entire side before moving to the other side, economy of effort.

Pillows were never allowed under the chin while changing pillow cases; this reduced the chances of contamination from a patient's disease.

Bottom sheets were to be tight enough for a coin to stand on them. I didn't know wrinkles in sheets caused bed-confined patients develop sores, decubiti.

Everyone knew we were the new students, probies. I wore my blue-and-white-striped dress and white-bibbed apron with pride. My head had no covering, though. It would be six months before I could earn my cap.

I felt stupid when Miss Whiteside pulled the sheets from a bed I had just completed and said, "Start over, Bobbie. It's not tight enough."

I looked at the poor patient sitting and looking at her clumsy student. I attempted an excuse, and she consoled me.

"Don't worry about it. They want you to know the right way. You'll thank them for this one day."

All beds weren't made the same way. An occupied bed was completed differently from an unoccupied bed. Patients, too ill to get up, were turned and positioned to allow removal of the linens with the least discomfort. I was glad we learned to complete an unoccupied bed first.

As I used my prayer routine, God began providing assistance at my every turn. Havoline Scott, a girl from Columbus, Georgia, was the smartest student of the class. One evening she said to me,

"Why don't you come down to my room and study with me tonight."

"All right," I said. I didn't intend to, though. What could she see in me? I certainly couldn't help her. I didn't realize God was giving me another helper. When I didn't come to her room, she came to mine. "Are you ready to study, Bobbie?" What could I say except yes.

That first evening, I realized I didn't know how to study. As I listened to Havoline, I heard her eliminating unnecessary material and deciding what was essential to know. During our studying, she recognized my strong and weak areas.

"Bobbie, you're good in anatomy and physiology, so try to answer all those questions. They'll make up for the chemistry equations you don't attempt."

She began teaching me how to study and how to answer test questions. The quantity of studying wasn't nearly as valuable as the quality of studying I soon learned.

During a conference with Miss Mosley, she said, "I've noticed you have little difficulty with anatomy and physiology. Why don't you try any of the chemistry equations?" I explained my cosmetology background in relation to my lack of experience in chemistry. She showed me a few tips she knew and encouraged me to try.

After the next exam, I said, "Havoline, I worked five of the equations correctly!"

"I told you, you could do it," she answered.

Miss Mosley turned out to be a wonderful freshman adviser. Her bark was just that, a bark. She didn't bite; her tests did the biting.

She had a way of relating medical conditions to

everyday situations. While lecturing about shock, she went off on a tangent about an old drunk getting stabbed and laying in the gutter.

My mind roamed from dream to dream. *I'll be home in less than two weeks. I wonder if Anthony remembers me. What can I afford to buy him for Christmas? Thank you, Father, for helping me elevate my grades.*

Before leaving for Christmas vacation, we had finals. Each test consisted of twenty to twenty-five legal-size sheets of paper. I was glad the tests weren't timed. I worked as rapidly as I could. On about page fifteen, I felt like screaming. A three-page situation involved that drunk in the gutter. Miss Mosley had used that method to present shock. She had discussed symptoms, treatment, complications, and countless other important factors while I dreamed. She hadn't been on a tangent. I paid dearly for daydreaming when I should have listened. Never would I repeat that mistake.

Everyone was excited about going home for Christmas and tense about making grades good enough to return. Grades were to be posted on the bulletin board outside the library at 2 PM.

Grace and I rested on our beds, talking about numerous things. A relationship that started out on a shaky foundation became one of trust and love. We wouldn't have known how to live with anyone else.

"Well, Roommate, I guess we'll go and see if we'll be coming back after Christmas," Grace said.

We put our uniform aprons back on and headed for

the elevator. Students crowded around the posted grades. We finally obtained a position allowing us to see the grades.

Someone asked, "Who's number one?"

The reply was "Havoline." Everyone expected her to rank first.

I looked for my number in the middle of the numbers. It wasn't there. I looked lower; it wasn't there. I checked the last few numbers; it wasn't there.

"Roommate, where are you?" Grace asked.

"I don't see my number. I must have forgotten it. I wrote it in a book. Wait for me. I'm going back and recheck it."

The number was correct. I must have overlooked it. I went back to the elevator. Havoline got off and asked, "Bobbie, where did you rank?"

"I don't know yet. I couldn't find my number."

"Come on, I'll go with you. It's down there."

We returned to the board, and Grace asked, "Roommate, what's your number?"

"I don't know if I want to tell you."

We were to keep the same number during the entire three years. They would always know where I ranked if I told.

"Come on, Roommate. Here I am," Grace said while pointing to her number.

"And I'm here," Havoline said.

I told the number, and Havoline said immediately, "Here you are, Bobbie."

"I don't believe it! I don't believe it!"

My number sat securely beneath Havoline's. I

ranked second highest in the class. Prayer, effort, and Havoline were a winning combination. My chest filled with pride. I could hardly wait to share the news with Mama. I would be coming back after Christmas.

5

The train swelled with Christmas travelers. We sat three to a seat from Saint Louis to Little Rock, Arkansas. Some stood. None of us minded. We were students going home.

"Hi," I said to Daddy as I approached him in the train station.

"Where's Anthony?"

"He's home."

We reached home, and I tried to answer everyone's questions. Jean wanted to know if I came to stay.

Anthony remained at Mama's knee. He looked at me but made no attempt to come near me.

Mama said, "Anthony, that's your mother. Give her a kiss." He didn't move.

I remembered Miss Mosley's advice. "Don't push him. Let him come around on his own. He may be frightened of you at first."

I was prepared. When I bought Anthony's Christmas toys, I bought a few extras to reestablish our relationship. I noticed he followed me from room to room but remained beyond my grasp.

"Jean, help me unpack," I said.

I let her get everyone's gifts and place them under the tree. Then I placed a cowboy on the bed. An Indian followed. A stagecoach and cowboy came out next.

My son found his legs and speech. In a flash, he stood with his hand resting on my knee as he asked, "Mommie, did you bring me these toys?"

"Yes, I did. Have you been a good boy?"

He nodded yes.

"Can I hug you?"

He nodded yes again.

Charles came over, but his visit changed nothing. I needed a full-time husband, and Anthony needed a full-time father.

My ten-day vacation flew by. I kissed Mama Daisy and Jean good-bye. Daddy, Mama, and Anthony were taking me to the train station.

"He'll be all right," Mama said. She knew I was having difficulty leaving Anthony again. She was no different. As she prepared to leave the train, tears started down her face. She wanted me to go, but she was having trouble saying good-bye this time.

"Roommate! Roommate! Where's my roommate?" I heard as soon as I reached the dorm.

I recognized Grace's voice and laugh. I ran down the hall to meet her. I had been anxious to go home and just as anxious to get back. I was in a hurry to graduate.

"McClendon's back! McClendon's back!" sounded throughout the halls the next morning. Upperclassmen spread the word about McClendon. The way they talked aroused my interest. This had to be an important person for so many people to talk about her.

I entered Nursing Arts class and saw a smiling, immaculate strange nurse standing at the front of the room.

"Good morning, Girls. I'm Thelma McClendon. I'm your Nursing Arts instructor. I've been on maternity leave."

She smiled, but the way she walked, stood, and talked cautioned me about her. She didn't have a "bark" as Miss Mosley, but I believed her to be just as crafty. My beliefs were proven as I completed her first exam. She wasn't giving any grades away. Nor was she going to spoon-feed us. I would work to the maximum for her.

She had lectured about the origin and formation of various medical terms. Not once did she mention putting those terms on our test.

"Mrs. McClendon, you didn't tell us we were going to have medical terminology on this test," we complained.

"Was I supposed to tell you?" she asked.

"If we had known, we would have studied," we replied.

"Darling, anything you hear in this classroom may appear on your test. I'm not going to tell you what to study. Just be prepared for anything."

I looked at *cephalalgia, hemoptysis,* and *hematemesis.* Prefixes and suffixes refused to be remembered.

I'll be ready for her next time, I thought. A hint to

the wise is sufficient, Mom said.

We went to the wards daily. We knew why everyone had wanted to know when we would begin
working. Instructors said we were getting clinical
experience; students called it hard labor, labor that
produced pride each time a new procedure was mas-
tered.

The morning I was to perform my first catheterization, I rushed to the ward. My hurry wasn't prompted by a desire to tackle the task. I wanted to be
through before Mrs. McClendon came to the unit. I
preferred having Miss Whiteside observe my performance.

Darling spoken by Mrs. McClendon meant you
were going astray. It wasn't a love word. We hated
to hear it. When we had practiced giving injections,
I heard her ask me, "Darling, what are you about to
do?"

"I'm going to give her an injection of 1cc of Normal Saline," I replied. It was wintertime, but I felt
perspiration drip from my back. My hands were
nearly as wet.

Esther Chandler was my best friend. I wouldn't
hurt her, too much, I hoped. She was going to inject
me when I finished. I didn't want her having anything to get even for.

I realized Mrs. McClendon had called me that
dreadful word *darling*. In my mind, I quickly re-
traced the steps of the procedure. I had selected the
correct site—the deltoid muscle, cleansed it with alcohol, and had not contaminated the needle.

Mrs. McClendon didn't say anything else, so I proceeded toward Esther's arm.

"Darling" came from her again. I stopped, and she asked, "Where is your medicine?"

I looked at the syringe. It was empty! My hands shook so badly that I pushed the medicine out when I picked up the syringe and had not realized it.

I found the patient I was to catheterize and introduced myself. Most of our patients were indigent. Indigents were to be treated as "kings and queens." Miss Whiteside taught us during our early days that the patient was the hub of everything we did.

After explaining that I was going to insert a small tube to get a urine specimen, I collected everything I needed and went to the bedside.

Miss Whiteside was observing a classmate doing her catheterization. Mrs. McClendon entered, smiling that crafty smile. I hesitated.

"Go ahead," she said. She stepped closer and adjusted the light.

"Can you see, Miller?" she asked.

"Yes."

"Where do you plan to insert?"

"Here," I said as I pointed toward the urinary meatus.

"Go ahead," she repeated.

I inserted the catheter and got a return of blood! No urine appeared. Sweat, not perspiration, popped out on my forehead. I looked at Mrs. McClendon. She smiled slightly. I felt she was saying to continue.

After pouring the urine into a sterile specimen bottle, I joined Mrs. McClendon at the nurse's station.

"Miller, you did fine."

"Why did I get blood?" I asked.

"Did you forget to read your patient's chart?"

"No, I didn't."

"What is her diagnosis?"

"Cancer of the bladder," I responded.

"That's correct. She has hematuria. What's that?" she asked.

I had studied my terms. I replied, "She has blood in her urine."

"That's right," Mrs. McClendon said.

The list of procedures we could perform grew; so did our self-confidence. We needed to believe we were achievers. The subjects were getting harder. I faced daily fights with microbiology, introduction to medical-surgical nursing, sociology, diet therapy, and the most important subject—drugs and solutions.

"Working the problems is not hard. Just work carefully. Usually, you add or subtract incorrectly. The problem is still wrong," a junior warned.

"Don't believe her. They are hard. Wait until Juliette Lee gets you in her apartment," another student said.

"What're we going to do in her apartment?" Grace asked.

Another junior laughed and said, "If you miss more than three problems, you'll find out. You have to stay with her until you can correct and explain every mistake you make."

Miss Lee was director of education and instructor for drugs and solutions. Her reputation was that her bark and bite were bad. She walked fast, talked fast, and worked problems fast too.

"Girls, you'll have an exam at the beginning of each class. The test will always consist of twelve problems. If you miss one problem, you get an *A*, two problems missed equal a *B*, three equal a *C*, and anything else is failing."

For nearly a week, we computed problems aloud. Miss Lee called different ones to solve problems.

"We will have our first test tomorrow," Miss Lee said.

Later that evening, I said, "Grace, are you ready for tomorrow?"

"I think I need to review some more," she answered.

"I do too. Let's work some," I said.

Later Grace said, "Roommate, it's nearly eleven o'clock! I'm going to bed. If I don't know enough by now, I'm not going to learn it. See you in the morning."

She cut her lamp off and was asleep within minutes. I looked at Grace and her side of the room. We were totally opposite, but we lived together in perfect harmony.

She seldom made her bed. Clothes hung in disarray from each half-opened drawer. Other clothes lay on the closet floor or in her chairs. Several times, Esther and Havoline helped me clean her half of the room.

"Oh, Roommate, how nice! You cleaned my room," she would say after returning from a visit home.

For a few days, the situation would improve. Then she was back to her old housekeeping ways. Our room looked like a line divided us straight down the center. We had no problems living together though. We were the only roommates to continue living together as originally assigned.

I cut my lamp off, and figures danced before my eyes in the darkness. Sometimes before daybreak, sleep came.

Miss Lee passed out the exams and instructed us to work rapidly but carefully.

"You'll have one hour to complete your test," she said.

A few days later, she returned our test papers. I watched the faces of each student as they reached for their papers. Hurt and shock registered on nearly every face except Havoline's.

"Mrs. Miller," Miss Lee called. I received my paper and opened it to see my score; I folded it again just as rapidly. The top of my test had -11 marked in red across the top. I only worked one problem correctly!

"I don't know why you had so much trouble. You would think they were hard to work," Miss Lee said to the class. She continued, "Look over your papers and find your mistakes. When you can correct them, come up and explain them to me."

Student after student tried to explain. Everyone had heard about going to Miss Lee's apartment. No one wanted to spend an evening figuring medication dosages.

"It's five o'clock," Miss Lee said. Ten of us still needed to explain our errors.

"Go to supper and come to my apartment tonight at 6 PM."

Grace and I went to supper. I felt terrible. I had about eight problems left to explain.

We reported to Miss Lee's apartment at the correct time and began where we stopped. Grace started explaining her errors.

Miss Lee said, "Grace, close your eyes."

Grace obeyed.

"Now, visualize the problem. Come on. Set it up correctly, first." She questioned, "What do you want to give? What do you have on hand? Your stock drug. Let's work the problem. You always have two known facts and one unknown. Come on, Grace. Keep your eyes closed!" Miss Lee said.

Grace began but failed to multiply her decimals correctly.

"Grace, you know that's wrong. Come on. Think!" Miss Lee commanded. "What do you see? Keep your eyes closed."

"Miss Lee, I can't see anything with my eyes closed but stars!" Grace giggled.

Miss Lee slapped Grace's hand and again commanded, "Think!"

We gained our freedom about ten o'clock that night. We had laughed and had fun, but I felt sad too. The hour was late, and I had other lessons to complete.

Grace didn't attempt to study.

"Roommate, I'm going to bed. I don't have time to worry about those problems. I'm too tired. You better go to bed too."

I didn't want to study, nor was I ready to sleep. It was time for prayer, "Father, I'm so tired. I must learn to work these problems. Help me understand and keep me alert for errors. I thank You, Father."

I received my second test paper and peeped at the score. Across the top was -4. I was on my way although success had not been reached yet.

The first six months were rapidly ending. Excitement and dread ran neck and neck. We would receive our caps within days or be told to go home.

I felt fairly secure because my grades had ranged in the *B* or *A* area. I became so adept at computing drug problems, I received several -0 papers. I was not required to take the final exam; I was exempted.

Several classmates went to class to take a "doomsday" exam. The results would determine whether they remained or went home. We waited upstairs for them because we were supposed to be learning the Nightingale Pledge. No one could study. We had friends downstairs fighting for survival. Most of us prayed they would work carefully. Carelessness was destroying them. Miss Lee said carelessness would be the difference between an alive patient and a dead one.

We lived on the same floor with the director of nursing. Miss Gore's apartment was around the corner from us, but she heard the shrieks and yells we made.

We closed the fire doors to keep our noise in with us when we lined up on the hall to dance. Everyone formed a line and danced the Madison. I couldn't sing, but I could dance.

Grace sang solo, but she had two left feet and no natural rhythm for dancing as most of us did. She tried, and we laughed until we cried. Our fun would grow loud enough to penetrate the fire doors.

"R-I-N-G! R-I-N-G!"

"It's the house phone." Someone inside the hospital or dorm was calling.

"Quiet! Be quiet!"

"Someone answer it."

"Hello. Just a minute. Mrs. Miller, it's for you."

"Who is it?" I whispered.

"It's the housemother" was whispered back.

"Be quiet," I warned again in a muted tone.

Everyone liked me and was good to me. Most thought I was mature and never dreamed I was in the center of any "loud fun."

"Mrs. Miller, Miss Gore called and said you all are too loud. Will you do me a favor? Take the names of anybody too loud." She wouldn't have to call again. She knew where to begin.

As soon as I hung up I said, "We've got to be quiet. She wants me to take names."

A brief pause ended our festive mood. Girls drifted off to the TV room, the kitchen, the laundry room, or went to Billy Burk's for a juicy hamburger.

The afternoon following doomsday exams, we sat around as if someone had died. No one laughed or yelled. Tears ran, and cries sounded throughout the hall. Four of our classmates failed and were packing to go home.

The week ended with us being ranked as we were

before Christmas. Grace ran up to me, took my hand, and pulled me to the elevator.

"Come on, Roommate," she said. "I want to show you something."

"What is it? Oh! I know! You remembered my number. I knew I shouldn't have told you."

We joined those crowded around the bulletin board, and someone said, "Congratulations, Bobbie." Grace pointed to my number. It didn't sit beneath Havoline's; it sat on top. I was number one. Havoline assumed second position.

Prayer and Havoline were my winning team. I hadn't stopped praying, and Havoline did an excellent job of teaching me how to study and take exams. I wrote to Mama:

> I wish you could come to Capping Ceremony, It's going to be beautiful. I can hardly wait to get my cap. We'll get our nurse's cape in a few days too.
>
> We aren't going to the wards now. We practice everyday for the program. It's a big occasion. I think the mayor will speak also.

The big night arrived, and everyone was spotlessly clean. Uniforms were without a wrinkle or crease, and shoes were gleaming white.

The moment of the evening had come. Amid glowing candles, we faced an auditorium filled with guests. In unison, we began:

> I solemnly pledge myself before God and in the presence of this assembly to pass my life in purity and to practice my profession faithfully. I will abstain from

whatever is deleterious and mischievous, and will not take or knowingly administer any harmful drug. I will do all in my power to maintain and elevate the standard of my profession, and will hold in confidence all personal matters committed to my keeping and all family affairs coming to my knowledge in the practice of my calling. With loyalty will I endeavor to aid the physician in his work, and devote myself to the welfare of those committed to my care.

I wondered how many in the audience knew the seriousness of the occasion. Did they realize what we pledged to do? Each of us knew. We had not gone to the wards because we explored the pledge to the smallest detail. Each unfamiliar word was defined. All instructors assisted in preparing us to recite during the program.

Summer vacation was upon us before we realized it. Again, I was anxious to see Anthony. He hadn't forgotten me. We did everything together. He wanted to follow me to Saint Louis.

"I promise, I'll come back for you. You be a good boy for Nannie."

"I want to go, Mommie," he cried.

I wouldn't have a hard time leaving him. I was in a hurry to complete the other two years. Two weeks of rest, and I began the ride back to Saint Louis.

My social life began bursting forth in every direction. Studying required less of my time. The subjects weren't easier, but I knew how to study and wisely use my time. My prayer routine was maintained too.

I was selected social committee chairman of the class and of the school. Dorothy Jackson had been correct about the availability of men. Planning activities to bring the opposite sex into our world was a constant endeavor.

Not being a "token" for a school needing to meet racial standards was a wise choice. I couldn't have met the men we were meeting. When I married the next time, I wanted a marriage meeting the words of our vow.

Men professional, nonprofessional, younger, older, handsome, not too handsome, and countless other descriptions—came and went in my life. They were everywhere, but the one for me remained undiscovered as graduation neared. I had to have a special man. He needed enough maturity to be a father to my young son.

"Come on, Roommate, let's go."

I opened my eyes and joined Grace at the elevator. We had been granted a fifteen-minute break. Most of my classmates spent their break time smoking or playing cards. I learned to sleep five or ten minutes and wake totally refreshed.

We no longer went to the wards. Junior and senior experiences were behind us. Our days were being spent in state board review. Each instructor came to class to review us in her specialty.

We were a close class until recent days. Tempers flared. Friendships grew cool. Grace and I had the distinction of being the only roommates to remain together the three years. She became a gift from God. He gave me stability by bringing her father, a Baptist minister, into my life.

Esther was no longer with me. I missed my best

friend. She had been one of God's gifts too. I never knew a black family like Esther's. They loved and enjoyed each other. The oldest girl was a professional married to a professional. The middle girl was a Catholic nun. I had never met a black nun. I spent many holidays with her family. They welcomed me and allowed me to see a life free of tension.

"I'm going to marry a Catholic," Esther said for three years. That's exactly what she did. Squire was everything she wanted. She planned to graduate the following year.

The more we reviewed, the shorter our tolerance grew.

"How will we learn all this stuff?" I asked Grace.

"You're supposed to know it," she replied.

"If I ever knew it, I've forgotten it now," I answered.

All of us felt the same. That's the reason tempers were short. No one wanted to fail, but how could we know what to study?

I called Mama. "Mama, we take state boards next week. Don't forget to pray for me. It's going to be rough."

The morning we left for Jefferson City, people came from everywhere to say good-bye. Midgie had bought an old model station wagon. Five of us, including Grace and Havoline, were riding with her. Our other classmates were taking the train.

We checked into the hotel and went out for food. No one intended to study. We brought no books. Grace expressed our feelings when she put her books away and said, "All I don't know I won't know. I'm not going to try to stuff my brain."

We returned to the hotel and saw people of every description overflowing into the lobby. Nursing schools throughout Missouri were represented.

As we dressed on the first test day, I began to feel sad, very sad. I started crying.

Grace asked, "Roommate, what is wrong with you?"

Between tears, I said, "I feel like I'm going to fail. I just know I am, Grace."

"What's wrong with you? If you think you're going to fail, I guess I don't need to go," she said. My tears stopped while we laughed.

After breakfast, we walked to the registration desk to show the proper credentials. No one was allowed in the testing area unless she had a self-portrait signed on the back by her director of nursing.

After showing my picture, I was given a number.

"Mrs. Miller, you will keep this number throughout the testing. Find the seat with the corresponding number. You are to occupy that chair during each test. Do you have any questions?"

"No."

"Good luck."

A few steps more, and I entered the test area. I hadn't expected so many people. The number at the hotel had been trivial compared to the group I faced. I located my seat.

We talked while waiting to begin. We sat side by side at long tables. A classmate could be seen only if I leaned over and looked down the table. About ten seats away I saw a known face. I had no idea where Grace or Havoline were.

Tests and pencils were issued.

"The test will begin shortly. Read your instructions carefully. Don't spend too much time on one question. Come back to it later. You'll have two hours for each test. If you have a question, raise your hand, and we'll come to you. You may leave the room when you are finished. I think that's all. Do you have any questions?" No one asked a question. "Good luck. You may begin."

I realized I had read eight questions without answering any. Mrs. McClendon warned us to expect to not know a few. How many was a few? I remembered test day at Saint Joseph. *I can't blank out again. I can't.* That old feeling of fear clutched me in the pit of my stomach. Nausea increased. *Am I going to start vomiting?* I looked around in time to see a nun praying and making the sign of the cross. *If she needs to pray, I can forget it,* I thought.

Instead of giving up, I returned to question one and put the things Havoline taught me into practice. I prayed as I began.

When we had review for the examinations, someone said, "Let's write the test."

"How?" I asked.

"It's easy. Grace, you remember questions one to six; Bobbie you remember seven to twelve; Havoline, you take thirteen to eighteen."

"I'll take" and "I'll take" began sounding from all areas of the room. Everybody wanted in.

During break, paper and pencils came from

purses. Questions were written before anyone smoked or took any refreshments. We would put all the sheets together when we reached the hotel.

"That test was harder than I expected."

"How did you do?"

"What did you answer for number ten?"

"Weren't the situations long?"

"It took me two hours to read the test. I didn't get to go back to any I left blank."

"I know I failed OB."

Doubt filled every conversation. Mrs. McClendon said medical Nursing was the backbone of all other branches of nursing. It was not my favorite subject. Listening to my classmates, I realized I had not answered enough questions correctly to pass.

"Grace, I've already failed Medical Nursing, so I'm going to enjoy tomorrow."

"Me, too, Roommate. It's too late to worry now."

Psychiatric Nursing Exam was the first test of the second day. Like in the old song, I was "like a child in wild anticipation." I entered nursing to become a psychiatric nurse. I expected the test to be a challenge.

I read the two-page situation and began marking the test sheet. My anticipation was correct. The test was tricky; its challenge increased my excitement as I continued to read.

"I know I passed that test," I said during break.

All of us were anxious to begin the last examination. Surgical Nursing. Medical Nursing, Pediatric Nursing, and Obstetrical Nursing had been completed the first day.

We returned to Homer G. to begin the last weeks of training. We were allowed to choose the ward we would return to for additional experience.

"I don't know where I want to work," I said. I planned to work in psychiatry, but we had no psychiatric unit.

"Which did you enjoy most during your clinical rotations?"

"All of them," I answered.

"You have to decide on one of them by morning," I was told.

In my junior year, I completed Pediatrics and Obstetrics. Medical Nursing II and Surgical Nursing II were completed during my senior year. My thoughts roamed back over those days.

The night I was to see my first delivery, I hurried through supper. I shook while changing my uniform for a scrub dress. Clothing worn outside the unit was not allowed in any area containing mother or baby. This reduced chances of infecting them.

When we arrived, the drama of birth had begun. Mrs. Blackwell, our instructor, introduced us to the team. She quietly explained the events taking place. We sat watching from our seats in the observation area.

"Push! Push, Mama!" the doctor commanded.

"O—O—O—Oh! "O—O—O—O—Oh!" the mother groaned.

"Push, again."

"O—O—O—Oh!"

"Stop! Don't push!" "Relax."

A beautiful doll-sized head had emerged and hung

oddly to one side. Seconds later, another contraction came.

"Push, Mama!"

One push, and a baby filled the doctor's hands.

I remembered the two deaths I later observed. Death from childbirth rarely happened. It did occur for a fourteen-year-old and a mother of three beautiful daughters.

I don't want to work with any part of Labor and Delivery, I decided.

Pediatrics had been a challenge. There was so much to learn. I couldn't begin learning the abnormal until I understood normal growth and development.

Mrs. Pearl Lee spit out growth and development as if it were stamped on her brain. I discovered I couldn't answer according to Anthony's development. I had to learn an acceptable range since children differed in their development.

Homer G. was filled with kids sick from nearly every ailment in the textbooks. I remembered some of the kids especially. There had been kids whose memory stayed with me. An eighteen-month-old baby was so severely burned that his fingers and toes began dropping off before he died; a five-year-old had screamed, "My head hurts!" An autopsy revealed cancer of the brain. I thought of the countless ones severely ill from diarrhea, starvation, child abuse, accidents, and birth defects.

No, I never want to work with children. They remind me of my own son too much, I decided.

I agreed with Mrs. McClendon—Medical Nursing

was a foundation to other branches of nursing. But I never intended to work on a medical floor. The people died too easily.

I considered gyn, GU, Orthopedics, and communicable Diseases. I eliminated them, too.

Then I remembered fun days in the operating room. Learning setups and instruments was not fun. Mrs. Bell had us draw and label each instrument. There must have been thousands! It was her method of teaching us to become efficient instrument nurses.

I laughed, remembering my first assist. I was to be suture nurse during a cholecystectomy. Instruments weren't my concern. I had other problems. I had to keep the surgeons supplied with thread to tie off blood vessels or to sew tissue when needed.

Thread looked like thread to me, but all thread is not alike. Thread sizes and types are the same as shoe sizes and styles in a shoe store. The surgeon called for size and type; I was to fill the request.

"I'll be there to help you," Mrs. Bell said.

I scrubbed and gowned in O.R. dress. While a classmate arranged her instruments, I opened the sutures and started arranging them as Mrs. Bell had taught.

The surgeon entered, and I realized Mrs. Bell wasn't ready! She hadn't scrubbed. She couldn't help us unless she had on sterile attire. My large eyes grew larger. Perspiration started down my face. I couldn't wipe it; I had on sterile gloves.

Mrs. Bell saw my fright. She came and wiped my wet forehead without touching any of my clothing. Then, very softly, she soothed me, "I'll be right here. I'll help you. It'll be all right. You can do it."

"Scalpel," the surgeon said.

My classmate slapped the knife into his hand as Mrs. Bell taught us to do. I watched blood appear at the slight skin opening. Watching ended for me seconds later.

"Tie," the surgeon requested.

"Tie," he repeated. His hand remained extended.

"Bobbie, give him a 4-0 black silk suture," Mrs. Bell said.

Lingo concerning sutures—chromic, cutting needles, skin needles, and sizes—was new to my ears. Matters were made worse because the entire surgical team was foreign. Between their accents and masks covering their noses and mouths, I couldn't understand anything they requested.

Mrs. Bell became my interpreter. Her presence carried me through the operation. When I finally felt secure enough to look at something other than my sutures, I saw the skin being closed. I had missed seeing the gallbladder being removed.

"The operating room is not my interest. I want my patients awake so we can talk."

Nothing was left, except the Surgical Service. It always was my second choice. Most of the patients improved after surgery and went home. That I liked. Remembering the days we carried bedpan after bedpan to female patients prompted me to choose Male Surgery. Men didn't like young females bringing or removing their bedpans.

Grace moved home as the other Saint Louis students did. It was strange living alone, but it would not be for long. We would become graduate nurses in one week.

Grace walked into the room as I dressed for our last day of clinical experience. Seeing her lifted my spirits. I was down, slightly. Some of these people I would never see again. My plans to go home remained firm.

We went to the ward and did nothing except say good-bye. We went to other wards saying good-bye also.

"Are you going to work at Homer G.?" was asked on each floor we visited.

The day seemed shorter than others. It ended as the clock clicked 3:15 PM. I turned to leave and felt hands grip me!

R—I—P! R—I—P! R—I—P!

A button popped. Another button popped. R—I—P! A long tear appeared in the sleeve of my dress. I began to run. I eluded one set of hands and fell prey to others. With most of my uniform showing large gaping holes, I headed for the tunnel. The day was hot, but I was too exposed to go to the dorm from the outside.

"Roommate!" Grace yelled.

All of us were heading for the tunnel. Our uniforms were streaming behind us in long tattered pieces.

"Grace!" I screamed back.

I had forgotten the custom of tearing uniforms from the backs of students as they completed their last student day. The hospital staff had remembered. It didn't take much effort to rip the cloth. Three years of constant wear caused uniforms to tear, normally. Everyone recognized senior students by the adhesive tape used to cover holes in uniforms.

When we reached the nurses' residence, few pieces of uniform were left. Undergarments were visible. We tore the last threads of our uniforms away as we rode up to the fifth floor.

I had a week to play since I had no makeup days to complete. No more signing in and out. I was free to come and go as I pleased. We partied for days. At times, I felt I was passing myself; I returned to change clothes so often. Mr. Right had not appeared yet, but I knew the qualities I wanted in my next husband. Charles and I had divorced at the beginning of my senior year.

Graduation Day I slept late. As noon approached, Havoline checked to see if I intended to eat lunch. I had showered and begun dressing when the tears started.

"Oh, Father, I'm so lonely. I'll miss everybody. I thank You for seeing me through these three years. I could never have done it without You. I wish Mama and Daddy could be with me tonight. Help me be strong enough to carry on alone."

I rode to Kiel Auditorium that night on a bus carrying the entire class and Miss Gore. We began with thirty-four students. Twenty-five were graduating. Everyone looked great in gleaming white uniforms. Never would we wear blue and white dresses and bibbed aprons again!

We were having a combined graduation with City Hospital. Their class was all white except for a few blacks. We were not strangers though. During our junior year, half of my class and half of their class became one class of psychiatric nursing students. We lived in their dorm at that time.

The first class had been scheduled to meet in Malcolm Bliss's auditorium. I had gulped breakfast in my haste to get to class. I had waited a long time to receive this training. I had entered the auditorium. An invisible line cut through the center of the room. Everyone on the left wore pink and was white. The right side was all black and wore blue and white.

A young, attractive, well-groomed black nurse had walked to the front of the room. "I'm Gladys Cox, your instructor," she had said.

While she had continued introducing the unit, I had tried to evaluate her. *She speaks softly, but she's no pushover. She's petite, so she can handle herself. If she couldn't, she wouldn't be working with mental patients. I bet she doesn't tolerate much. I'll have to watch myself,* I had thought.

Later, I had learned that Mrs. Cox was a graduate of Homer G. That had been an added incentive to study and stay out of trouble. Being a good student had allowed me to get away with pranks, most of the time. I had not been sure about her. She had been too quiet for me to really evaluate.

As days grew into weeks, I had realized Mrs. Cox's wiseness. She had seen how divided we were the first few days but had said nothing. No problems had developed because she had taught theory and had left race relations for us to settle.

We had been divided into groups of six or eight. Three of us and three of them had been assigned to work together. Daily contact had quickly removed barriers of mistrust.

I stepped from the bus and caught a glimpse of Mrs. Cox. I would miss her. She had been everything I hoped a psychiatric instructor would be. Because she was a graduate of Homer G., she gave us no slack. We had to dig for each passing grade. She certainly didn't allow me much room to pull my antics. I remembered the incident over *Snake Pit*.

I had wanted to watch *Snake Pit* while on duty. I had found Mrs. Cox and said, "Mrs. Cox, may I watch *Snake Pit?*"

"When?" she had asked.

"When it comes on this morning."

"Bobbie, you need to be talking with your patient. She's pretty sick."

"I know. That's why I need to see *Snake Pit*. It'll help me to know how to help her. She's a schizophrenic just like the people in the movie."

"No, I don't think you should," had been the final answer.

I had wanted to see *Snake Pit*. My patient was nearly catatonic. Anywhere I placed her, she would remain. I had asked her, "Would you like to see *Snake Pit?*"

She hadn't answered. I would have been shocked if she had. She hadn't said she didn't want to see it, either.

I had guided her to the couch and had sat beside her as I watched the movie. Mrs. Cox couldn't have said anything if my patient had wanted to see the movie. I had been meeting the requirement of observing my patient and attempting to interpret her behavior.

The movie had ended, and Mrs. Cox had asked me to come to her office. My boldness had deserted me as I followed her. Her voice had remained calm, but for thirty minutes she had asked me enough questions about catatonics and schizophrenics to last me a lifetime. I didn't disobey her again.

"Bobbie," someone called as I lined up for the processional. It was Margaret. She was a strange white girl. She had refused to let me snub her. The harder I tried, the more she seemed to be unaware of my feeble attempts. We became close friends while working at Bliss.

The main speaker neared the end of his address. I glanced around and saw relatives and well-wishers throughout the auditorium.

I wish Mama and Daddy could be sitting here now. I promised to make them proud of me, and I'm keeping that promise. Thanks to You, God.

Clap! Clap! Clap!

Awards time was about to begin. We debated several days about who would receive Most All Around Student Award. My name was "kicked around" more than once.

"It gives me pleasure to award the Most All Around Student with a two-hundred dollar scholarship to assist with continued study. Will Bobbie Jean Miller come forward, please?" Miss Gore said.

I didn't move. I heard her, but it couldn't be true!

"Roommate, go on!" Grace called to me.

Connie Fitzpatrick, class president, said, "I told you, it was Bobbie. It had to be her."

I approached Miss Gore as the applause thundered. No one knew how near tears I was. Nor did they know how proud I was. My award was another way of saying thank you to Mama.

6

I had discussed going home with Havoline for a few days, but thoughts of my little chocolate son were drawing me back to Fort Worth. We had so much fun after graduation, I nearly spent all my money. I would have to leave for Texas very soon or find a job.

The day I departed, Grace and Havoline were at my side. I wanted to go, but I wanted my friends too. I boarded the bus (didn't have money for the train) and watched my friends getting smaller as the distance grew between us. Tears stung my eyes.

It was time for a pep talk. *No looking back, Bobbie Jean Miller. That chapter of your life is complete. Look ahead to your unwritten future. You have a son to get to know!*

Thoughts of Anthony grew with each turn of the wheels. I couldn't get home soon enough. My baby was waiting for me.

I had not told anyone when to expect me, so I took a cab home. I was already using my wings of maturity.

"Mommie! Mommie!" Anthony screamed as I exited from the taxi. How different from my first return.

"Mommie, are you home to stay?"

"Yes, Anthony, I'm home to stay."

"Will you take me next time, Mommie?"

"If I ever leave home again, I'll take you."

Mama had done a beautiful job of rearing Anthony, but I was more than ready to assume my responsibility. How could I ever repay her for everything she had done for me?

Tears and hugs came as I showed everyone the letter I received graduation night.

"I knew my little girl could do it!" Mom said. Nothing had changed. Her belief in me was as strong as ever. "It was hard, at times, but it was worth it, Bobbie."

"You will be able to provide for yourself and your son. You'll find another husband one day. You won't have to take the first one coming by either. You can afford to be selective," Mama teased.

"When are you going to work? Tomorrow?" Daddy teased.

"No, she needs a rest," Mama said. "She's worn-out. Take a month or two before you think of working."

I was unbelievably tired. For several days I slept, ate, and renewed my acquaintance with my son. It felt good being home.

Before the month ended, I wanted to work. I didn't go to school for three years to sit around the house.

"I think I'll start looking for a job today," I said.

"Are you sure you're ready? You don't have to rush into working," Mom said. "Where do you want to work?" she asked.

"I still want to work with mental patients."

"I told you three years ago to start with your father," she said.

I was proud of Daddy. He hadn't had one drink in six months, I was told.

"I wrote the United States Public Health Service Hospital," I said.

"The what?"

"Everybody calls it the Narcotic Farm."

"Where is it?"

"I'm not sure, but it's here in Fort Worth."

"How did you hear about that place?" Daddy asked.

"Do you remember Mr. Denson, my seventh grade teacher?"

"Yes."

"He had a twin brother, who worked there. He brought a patient to visit our class, once. Mama, you should have seen him. A grown man playing with his cap like a small boy. I never forgot him, so I wrote and asked about working there."

"Did you get an answer?"

"Yes, I was suppose to go for an interview and have my name added to a waiting list. I didn't get to go for the interview; I was still in Saint Louis."

"Maybe, it's not too late," Mama said.

"I don't know. The letter said I had two weeks to reply. I knew I wouldn't be home in time, so I didn't answer."

Mama said, "Go ahead and call. It doesn't cost anything to call."

I made the call and was instructed to come for an interview the next day.

"Mama, I got the job!" I said as soon as I returned from the interview. "It's such a large place. It's not one building like most hospitals. It has about five or six buildings. I talked with the director of nursing too. A Mrs. Ous. Ousta; I can't remember her name. I start working Monday morning at eight."

I had not heard anything about the results of my State Boards. I would be working as a Graduate Nurse until I heard. The director made it clear, I couldn't continue working if I failed to receive my license. If I passed, I didn't have to get a Texas license as long as I remained in Federal Service.

"What are you doing?" Mama asked.

"I'm trying to decide which uniform to wear in the morning."

"I like this one," Jean said.

"I don't know. What do you think, Mama?"

"How many uniforms have you bought? And look at these prices. You're suppose to be working."

"I want to be one of the best dressed G.N.'s that hospital ever saw."

Jean asked, "What's a G.N.?"

"A Graduate Nurse. I've graduated, but I'm not registered yet. Mama, you never did say which uniform you like."

She closed her eyes and reached out. When her hand touched one, she said, "I like this one." I manipulated the dresses so she touched Jean's choice.

Monday morning I sat in the personnel office ready for duty I thought. At eleven o'clock, I was still in Personnel. My eyes were tired of reading and my hand was tired of swearing. Why would I want to overthrow the government? I didn't intend to bring anyone anything, so I didn't clutter my brain with the list of things considered contraband.

As noon neared, Mrs. Myers said, "I'll take you to Nursing Service. Come back here when you finish lunch. We're almost through."

Mrs. Day, the assistant director of nursing, walked nearly as fast as Mom. She escorted me to lunch. I didn't dare allow my steps to fall behind hers.

The entire hospital was connected by a tunnel network. Each building could be reached without going outside. Men—men—men! Everywhere I looked, men were walking in that tunnel. I felt uneasy around so many men.

"Mrs. Miller, we house nearly a thousand men here. We have two services, Neuropsychiatric Services I and II. Mental patients and addict patients are not placed together. Have you had much experience with addict patients?"

"No. I saw only two while I was a student."

"You'll be assigned to our Infirmary Ward first, but you'll be oriented to each ward before you're given a ward assignment."

Around two o'clock I heard the magic words, "We'll take you to your ward now. Report there in the morning at 6:45."

Mrs. Day walked her fast pace with me nearly trotting at her side. She wasn't about to leave me alone in that tunnel.

R-i-n-g! R-i-n-g!

We waited at a grill gate for someone to answer our ringing. A man dressed in a white shirt and pants responded to our ring. He unlocked the grill door, and we entered.

"Mrs. Miller, I want you to meet the nurses you'll be working with. This is Mrs. Ricketts, the Head Nurse. This is Mrs. Groce and Mrs. Hastings, the Staff Nurses. I'll leave you with them."

While we ate that evening, Mama pressed for news about my first day. I hadn't told her much because I was trying to assimilate the events of the day. It would be a long time before I settled down to working in one unit. What if they put me on an addict ward?

I think I'll quit, crossed my mind each day for weeks. I wanted to work with mental patients who had a chance to go back to their communities. The ones on the Infirmary Ward were mostly very old central nervous system lues victims. Some were first hospitalized before I was born! Such a high price to pay for contracting syphilis before a cure was discovered. The effects were not reversible.

Each time I thought of quitting an inner impulse urged me to hang on. I began rotating to other units, and my hope began growing. Each unit was unique. On one, I enjoyed group therapy sessions; on another I learned while assisting with electric shock therapy;

and on another, attending team meetings was the highlight of the unit.

As I prepared for work one morning, I noticed that Mom remained in bed. That just wasn't like her. I didn't want to face the obvious—Mama's physical health was deteriorating.

Severe hypertension had plagued her for ten years. Her blood pressure reading was so elevated nurses called other nurses to check their results. Mama's normal pressure ranged in the stroke area for most people. Dr. Stow tried everything to lower the pressure. It would decrease for a while, then return to its elevated state.

During my second year of nursing, Mama had had severe hemorrhages from the nose. Nell, Mama's childhood playmate and still best friend, had called me.

"Bobbie, I think you need to come home. Your mother went into the hospital, nearly, as soon as you left."

"What's wrong with her?"

"She's had terrible hemorrhages from her nose. They get them stopped then they happen again. She didn't want me to call you, but I think you should know."

"I'll be home as soon as I can get there."

I had hung up in tears. Grace had been at my side instantly. She had taken control. No transportation would have been leaving Saint Louis before morning. I had no money, but the school had supplied me with a loan. All I had to do was wait for morning.

"Can Mama hold on?" had been my unspoken question.

Grace had encouraged me to believe. "She'll be all right, Roommate. You'll get home in time."

I had remained home two weeks, providing Mom's care and taking over household chores. I had wanted to stay, permanently. No school was more important than Mama.

She had insisted, "Bobbie, if you really want to make me happy, go back to school. We'll make it until you finish."

She had paid a costly price for me to complete my education. I had become aware of the frequent complaints of pain radiating down Mom's entire left arm. The pain hadn't lasted long. She had considered the pain an annoyance; I had known from her description that she was having cardiac decompensation. Her heart wasn't able adequately to pump the needed amount of blood.

Mama looked young for her forty-five years. While my weight increased, she maintained her shapely 118 pounds. Nearly all of her hair was still black. I was looking on the outside, though. Inside, Mama was sick; sick enough to have received a permanent disability rating the year I graduated from high school.

I went into her bedroom and asked, "What's wrong, Mama? It's not like you to stay in bed."

"I've been awake nearly all night." She clutched her chest and said, "I have a sharp pain here, and I'm so short of breath."

I saw she couldn't breathe deeply. She took short pants.

"You need to go to the doctor," I said.

"Maybe it'll go away. I hate to bother anyone."

"I'll stay home today. Let me call in."

I sat in the waiting room with Mama. My thoughts were alive with prayer. *Please God, let me be able to be good to Mama. I want to give her so much. Now that I'm making money, I can give her nice things. Spare my mother, please.*

While Mama dressed after an examination and chest X ray, Dr. Stow talked with me in his office.

"She's had a spontaneous pneumothorax."

He didn't attempt to explain the medical jargon. He expected me to understand, and I did. I couldn't understand how Mama's lung collapsed without causing more symptoms. At the moment, I wanted to know how it would re-inflate.

"Keep her on bed rest, and it should re-inflate on its own," he advised.

Mama's condition stabilized, and I began enjoying my job. Mrs. Oustaian called me and asked, "Mrs. Miller, have you heard from the State Nursing Board yet?"

"No, I haven't."

"You do understand, you can't continue working without a license."

"I know."

"We'll wait a few weeks more."

The following week, I arrived from work, and Mama handed me my mail. Then she said, "I have a surprise for you."

"What is it?" I asked.

She pulled another envelope from behind her back. "Guess who this is from."

"I don't know." I wasn't expecting any special letter. I had continued corresponding with Grace, Havoline, and Esther, so to hear from them wouldn't be a surprise. *Who could have written?*

"Mama, I can't guess."

"I should make you pay to get it, but I guess I'll give it to you," she said.

One glance at the return address and I lost my appetite. My state board results were inside that envelope. I started to open it, then decided against it. "I'll eat first," I said. I put the letter aside and went to the kitchen.

I needed time to think. *What reason can I use for failing my boards? What if I have to return to Missouri to retest? What if I can't pass on the second try? It's going to be embarrassing to tell Mrs. Oustaian I failed. Even more embarrassing when the staff hears of my failure.*

I picked at my food, trying to find an excuse that wouldn't hurt Mama too much. I finished moving the food around my plate and Mama asked, "Are you going to open your letter now?"

"I think I'll make you pay to see the results," I teased. "How much will you pay?" My attempts to be light-hearted allowed me to stall longer.

Daddy knew what I was doing. He insisted, "Stop stalling. Give us the bad news."

"What you mean, bad news? My baby has good news," Mama gushed.

I took a deep breath and ripped the envelope open. Carefully, I removed the contents. I wanted to see "350" written five times. Anything under 350 was failure. I wouldn't mind getting my license "by the skin of my teeth."

"Mama, look at this! All right! I've got to call Grace!"

"What is it? What did you make?"

"I needed 350 to pass. To make in the 600s is excellent. The 500s are very good. Mama look! My lowest grade is 597!"

I threw her the grades and my license, while I dialed the long distance operator. I needed to share the good news with my roommate.

Grace and Havoline had passed too. The news was already out in Saint Louis about how well I had done. I didn't know the instructors received the results before we did. We talked about the results of everybody else. When told that four of the class failed, my elation decreased slightly.

"Roommate, who has the test we wrote?"

"I don't know," Grace answered.

"Find out and give it to them for a review."

Some people never learned to successfully take an exam. The four failing were excellent nurses. One had been an *A* student. Maybe she blanked out as I did at Saint Joseph.

After report the next day, I said to Mrs. Ricketts, "I need to go see Mrs. Oustaian." I couldn't settle down to patient care until I told her of my success. I felt great writing *R.N.* behind my name. I was on my way up.

That night I finished reading Anthony his bedtime story, kissed him good night, and tucked him in. I wasn't sleepy. I thought about my life. I had a responsible position; was making an adequate income; had more clothes, expensive clothes, than room to hang them; and was saving money to buy a car. Life was not totally blissful, though.

"Mr. Right" had not come alone. I didn't see any way to meet him if I continued living as I did. I needed to start going where men were in numbers. Working 3 to 11 PM each weekend hampered my progress.

The following Saturday, a black after-five dress and black silk sandles went with me to work. I had permission to get off duty at 9 if everything were quiet. I hurried through my duties. After completing the Nursing Report, giving and charting all medications, and giving a report to the nurse relieving me, I changed my clothes.

A new club was in town. This was certainly a new Bobbie Miller. I had been to few clubs and never alone. I found the club. Cars parked bumper to bumper as far away as a block. Excitement overpowered uncertainty.

I entered a beautiful building and allowed my eyes to adjust to the dimmed lighting. Loud sounds of music quickened my desire to dance. The dance area was huge. It had to be to accommodate so many couples.

"Is that Mrs. Miller?" someone asked.

A male voice answered, "Yes, that's her." I looked

around and saw Jane and Marshall Batts. They were psychiatric attendants where I worked.

"Mrs. Miller, didn't I see you on duty this evening?" Jane asked.

"You sure did."

"What are you doing here? You didn't work days with us."

"I took annual leave."

"You did what?"

"I've got to get back into circulation. I've been working and spending all my time with my family. It's time to find male companionship. My son needs a father."

"You're around men all day."

"I'm not interested in patients, and so far I haven't seen any staff to interest me."

"Are you alone?" Jane asked.

"Yes, didn't you hear me say I'm looking for 'Mr. Right'?"

"Come sit with us . . ."

As I crawled into bed in the early morning hours, I reflected on the entire evening. I had danced and danced and had talked with fellows in my high school graduating class. *The evening was a success*, I thought.

Three months later, I was taking Annual Leave at least twice a month. To the clubs I went. Mrs. Day approached me one evening.

"Mrs. Miller, I have noticed you take Annual Leave at least twice every month. Don't you ever intend to let your hours accumulate? Is it really necessary for you to be off, so often?"

"Yes, it is."

"Well, you need to try to accumulate some hours."

I walked to the ward thinking, *Why should I accumulate leave time? I need to use my hours now. If I didn't have to work every weekend, I wouldn't need Annual Leave. This scheduling stinks. I'm not waiting eighteen months to get Saturday and Sunday off. When I do get those days, it'll be only for three months. Why don't they schedule like other hospitals? Staff nurses need one weekend a month.*

My efforts to find "Mr. Right" hadn't been fruitful. I met lots of fellows, as I had in Saint Louis. None appeared to possess fatherly qualities. I was tired of looking too. I stopped going out and began praying for "Mr. Right" to be brought into my life.

"Bobbie. Bobbie," someone called.

I looked around. "Beverly," I said.

"Where have you been?" she asked.

"I've been back in Texas about seven months. I went to nursing school in Saint Louis. What have you been doing?"

"Working is about all," she answered.

My uncle had married her aunt, so we grew up saying we were cousins. Our common love of roller skating and dancing added to our closeness.

"What are you doing this weekend?" she asked.

"I'm seldom off on weekends, but I will be off every weekend for the next three months."

"Good. Let's go out tomorrow night."

"All right."

That meeting began a weekly routine. Each weekend we attended a party or a club. We were always in search of a good time and a good male. I didn't want to remain a single parent, nor did I want a living-together relationship. Plenty of men were available, men looking for working women. I didn't need another dependent, either.

Beverly brought me home around three o'clock one Sunday morning. "What are you doing tonight?" she asked.

"I'm too tired to do anything. I'm going to stay home and go to bed."

"Go to bed now and sleep all day. You'll be ready by tonight."

"I can't. In a few hours I'll be in church with Anthony.

I believed Anthony needed a Christian foundation. I remembered going to church with Daddy. Sunday School and missionary societies interested me; I wasn't active in either.

All of us went to church that day. I was tired, but the sermon held my attention.

"I'm going to bed. I'm too tired to stay up a minute longer," I said after supper.

"Bobbie. Bobbie. Bobbie, wake up, Beverly is here."

No, it's not true. I'm dreaming. I don't have to get up. Mama shook me and repeated, "Beverly's here."

I wouldn't get any sleep unless I went to see what Beverly wanted. I went to the living room and saw my radiantly smiling cousin. How she could keep such hours and look so good was beyond my understanding.

"Everybody's going to the American Legion tonight."

"Beverly, I'm too tired to move. If everybody flew
to heaven tonight, I might have to push myself to
make the trip."

"Come on, Bobbie. We'll come home early."

"Beverly, I'm not kidding. I'm too tired to dress."

"Come on. This might be the night you meet 'Mr.
Right'."

"Even, 'Mr. Right' can't revive the dead!"

"Come on. If you really don't want to stay, we will
leave early."

"Is that a promise?"

"It's a promise. Want to shake on it?"

Two hours later we joined four other girls and
went to the American Legion. We found a table and
sat waiting for the band to begin playing. The club
began filling.

"Hi, Joe."

"Hi, Joe."

"Hi, Joe."

All my companions spoke to this fellow as he was
about to pass our table.

"Hi, there," he said.

Beverly asked, "Are you alone tonight?"

"Yea, I'm alone."

"Don't forget to come dance with me," Beverly
said. "Me too," the other girls said.

As promised, Joe asked Beverly, and anyone else
wanting to dance, to dance with him. He was an
excellent dancer. I didn't know him and was too tired

to make any efforts to meet him. I sat quietly waiting to escape to my bed.

"Hi, there, Wall Flower," Joe said to me.

"Hi," I said as coldly as possible.

"What's the matter? Did you lose your boyfriend?"

"No, I didn't." I could see he was conceited, egotistical, vain, arrogant, and narcissistic. My companions liked him; I didn't.

"You must not know how to dance."

"I can dance. I don't want to. I'm too tired."

"You can tell me the truth. You just can't dance, can you?"

"For your information, I'm a very good dancer."

"Let's dance!" he said.

I followed him, and soon we moved to the beat of rhythm and blues. The song ended, and we stayed to dance the next two songs also.

Joe escorted me back to my seat and promptly moved the person sitting next to me. He placed his glass there, located a chair, squeezed it into the small space beside me, then sat in the seat.

"You can dance, so you must have lost your boyfriend. I don't know anything else to make someone look as sad as you," he said.

"I told you, I'm tired. Beverly and I were out until three this morning. I just want to go to bed."

"Tell me anything. What are you drinking?"

"Coke," I replied.

"Let's dance," he said after ordering another Coke for me.

The remainder of the night, Joe sat by my side and

danced only with me. My companions didn't ask for any more dances.

"Good night, ladies and gentlemen. Thanks for coming and come again," the M.C. said.

Joe said, "Let's go get a cup of coffee."

"I don't want coffee," I answered.

"Well, let's go talk."

"We've been talking all night."

"I can't talk to you in front of all these girls."

"You've been doing a pretty good job of it."

"Come on. I'm not going to try anything funny."

"I don't want to. I'm going home."

"Beverly, tell your cousin, I'm an all-right fellow. She won't go get a cup of coffee with me."

Beverly looked at him, then at me. She grinned while forming a facial expression that said, "I can't make her do anything." Joe left, and we stood outside talking to another girl we had met. Beverly knew someone anywhere we went.

Arlene said, "I've invited some friends over for a few drinks. Why don't you all come too. I just live two blocks from here."

Beverly said, "All right, we'll come for a little while."

I wanted to go home, but she was driving. I lived miles from where we were. I wouldn't be a party-pooper. *If I ever get home, I'm going to stay there. I'm tired of this life,* I thought.

Shortly, after 2:30 the front door opened. In walked Joe! "Hi," he said. Then he saw me. Straight as an arrow flying to a target, he came to me.

"What are you doing in my house?"

"I didn't know you lived here."

"Yes, you did. Why didn't you say you wanted to come home with me?"

"I'm here because of Beverly."

"Tell me anything," he said.

Beverly joined us and said, "I'm not ready to go. I know you need to get home. Is it all right if Joe takes you?" Before I could answer she continued, "Joe, will you drive her home for me?"

"Yes, I'll take her."

We drove and exchanged light conversation. His name was not Joe; it was Bernard Jobe. He was divorced and in no hurry to find another Mrs. Jobe. I answered his questions concerning my vital statistics. We reached home; I thanked him and dismissed him from my thoughts.

Mama was awake. She said, "I thought you were coming home early."

"I did too. You know Beverly when she gets out. I think I've had it with these late hours."

Mama said nothing, but I knew she would be happy if I did stop the late hours.

"Don't wake me tomorrow. Correction, today. I want to sleep until time to dress for work. Try to keep Anthony entertained, please."

Surely, it's not time to go to work. Didn't someone call my name? Was I dreaming?

"Bobbie. Bobbie," Mama called. I peeped at her with one eye.

"You have company," she said.

"Who is it?"

"I don't know. It's a young man."

"What time is it?"

"It's 12:15."

"Who's coming to visit this time of day?"

"I don't know, but you need to get up and find out."

I threw on a robe, removed the hair curlers, washed my face and brushed my teeth. All the time, I thought of getting back to sleep. I didn't intend for my visitor to visit long.

I went to the living room. Bernard Jobe sat in the center of the couch! I had not had my usual one cup of coffee; seeing him produced better results.

"Hi, Bobbie."

"Hi," I said.

"I know you're surprised to see me, aren't you?"

"I never considered you when Mama said I had company."

"I was on my lunch break, and I thought I'd come by."

For thirty minutes we talked. He wasn't all the names I considered the first night, maybe, just a little arrogant. Before leaving, he asked,

"What time do you get off work?"

"Eleven-fifteen."

"Will you have a cup of coffee with me one night?"

"I guess so."

"When?"

"Whenever you want to," I replied. "But not tonight. I need to get some sleep."

"Tomorrow night?"

"All right."

After discussing the place and time of our meeting, he was gone.

"Who was that?" Mama asked.

"I met him last night. His name is Bernard Jobe."

"He looks like a nice fellow."

"How can you tell by looking? How do you like him and dislike Tony?"

"You know, Tony is not your type. He's a hoodlum."

"You're right, Mama. I don't ever plan to see him again. Maybe I can get another half hour of sleep."

I kept the appointment with Bernard. He was different from other fellows I dated. He was mature and knew what he wanted out of life. We agreed to go out Saturday night.

Our Saturday date led to three months of constant dating. I dropped the other fellows. It was great not having to keep those late hours.

"Did I hear you correctly?" I asked.

"Yes, you did," Bernard answered.

"No, you didn't say what I thought you said. You told me you weren't looking for a wife."

"It's been a lot of water under the bridge since then. I'm going to marry you."

I laughed and laughed. No words came. I didn't know what to say.

"What's so funny?" he asked.

"Are you serious?"

"Do you see me laughing?" He wasn't laughing. He was serious. "Will you marry me?" he asked.

"I guess so. Yes, I will." The engagement was sealed with a kiss.

That night, I thought about my relationship with the man I would marry in a few months. Prayer had worked in school, so I prayed every night that God would send "Mr. Right" into my life. I hadn't considered Bernard a candidate, but he was the one sent.

We were a perfect match. Besides dancing, we enjoyed doing things that included Anthony and Jean. I noticed Bernard didn't give in to Anthony's acting-out. He held him in control. He was the answer to my prayers.

"I'm glad you're getting married," Mama said when I told her. "You're going to need a man to help you raise Anthony."

"She has me," Daddy said.

"You know your Daddy. You need dependable help," Mama responded.

"We're going to buy a small home. We save one hundred-twenty dollars every month."

"Who's the banker?" Daddy asked. "I am," I said.

Mama said, "You better keep your money in a secure hiding place. I'd hate for you to find it gone when you need it. Your father will borrow from anybody once he starts drinking. He hasn't had anything in about six months. He may get a big thirst any day now."

"No. No, I'm through doing that. I don't have to take anything. My daughter will give me a loan if I need one."

Mama looked at me with her beautiful large expressive eyes and said, "Did you hear him?" We both laughed. Daddy never repaid either of us.

I walked around on a cloud of happiness, as our

wedding date approached. Everyday, I looked at my baby blue dress, shoes, and hat I planned to wear.

"What about your bouquet?" Mama asked.

"I'm carrying the small white Bible I received the night I got my nursing cap. It'll have tiny red roses covering the front."

"Have you finished addressing the invitations?"

"I put them in the mail box yesterday. What else?"

"Do you have everything for the reception?"

"Check. May I wear your pearls? They can be the something old and borrowed."

"Sure you can. I guess you're ready. If you aren't, you have two weeks to discover anything forgotten."

"Mama, I can hardly wait."

My cloud of happiness gathered into a thunderhead. One evening at work, an attendant called me aside.

"Mrs. Miller, have you heard what's being said?" Mr. Greg asked.

"About what?"

"Well, the hospital grapevine says you have been sexually involved with some of the addict patients."

"What!"

"I didn't believe it, but I thought you should know."

"What was I supposed to be doing?"

"Something about being in the addict patient's rooms."

"I'm supposed to be in their rooms. How can I take care of them, if I don't go inside the room? (I was assigned to Infirmary again.) Maybe, I should stay at my desk and let them come to me."

"Settle down. Cool down. I didn't believe it."

"You said the grapevine had it. Some of these people live from day to day to tell what they heard or think. Once a lie starts, it's like a brush fire."

Everytime someone looked at me, I thought, *They're thinking I'm like the nurses caught doing those things.* I wanted my supervisor to hurry and come. I planned to quit.

Miss Turner finally arrived. I told her everything Mr. Greg said, and she laughed. That's correct—laughed.

"Honey, I don't believe what I hear out here. If I did half the things I'm supposed to have done, I wouldn't be working now. Forget it. Somebody's probably mad because you didn't let him do those things."

Laughing, she started making rounds. "Forget it."

I got off duty and started home. Mr. Greg's words turned over and over in my thoughts. I had been sentenced without a trial. In tears, I drove to Bernard's house.

"Bobbie, what's wrong with you?" I told him all the details. He patiently listened.

"Are you guilty, Bobbie?"

"How can you ask me that?"

"People are going to talk. They talked about Jesus Christ, and He wasn't guilty of anything. You know you aren't guilty. Why are you talking about quitting? I wouldn't quit. They would have to prove I was guilty. I'd make them fire me."

The thunderhead disappeared by the time I began

my drive home. My feet weren't completely back on a cloud of happiness, though.

The next day, I started my rounds after getting report. Another attendant approached me.

"Mrs. Miller, I think you should let me go with you. You don't need to go in addict rooms alone."

"Why?"

"You can't trust them. Especially, behind closed doors." He attempted a grin.

"You've heard the rumor, too, haven't you?"

"Yeah, but I don't believe it."

"Why don't you follow me in the mental patient's room? A crazy man may attack me. No one's trying to prevent that. No one has asked if the rumor's true. Why would I do that, anyway?"

"I just said, 'You need to be careful.' "

"Careful about what? When I start giving out sexual favors, it won't be for canteen scrip."

My outburst stopped the rumor.

December 14, 1963, arrived. I rose and prepared for a busy day. My feet "lightly tipped above the cloud of happiness."

"In a few hours, I'll be Mrs. Bernard Jobe," I said to Jean. "It's his birthday too."

After completing last-minute preparations for the ceremony, I went home to prepare myself. Mama was still in bed.

"Mama, it's after four. The wedding starts at seven. You better get started."

"Baby, I don't think Mama can make it. I'm too weak. Go ahead without me."

"If you don't go, I don't go. I'm not going to marry unless you're there."

I took a seat opposite her bed and silently prayed she could go.

"Go ahead. Jobe is a good man. You'll need him when I'm gone."

"Mama, stop talking like that."

"I'm happy knowing you have security."

I refused to move from my seat. Finally, Mama requested, "Help me get dressed."

Daddy, Mama, Mama Daisy, Jean, and Anthony were dressed and in the car before I left the house.

"Get in," Daddy motioned.

I stood on the sidewalk, trying to decide how I could ride without mussing my dress.

"I don't want to wrinkle my dress."

"Get on top of the car," Daddy joked.

"Jean, you and Tony come up here with us. That'll give you more room," Mama said.

Daddy drove and I thought some of the weirdest thoughts. *What if he's not there? How will it feel to be jilted?*

We arrived and Mama Daisy said, "Come on. People are already here." We were marrying at Dale's house. She was Bernard's cousin and pianist for the wedding.

"Go in, Jean, and see if he's here," I said.

She returned seconds later and said, "He's here."

Penny, Bernard's brother-in-law and best man, nervously laughed. "Let's get the show on the road," he said in his stuttering manner.

Alma Tate, my bridesmaid, grinned her usual

happy smile. "You ready, Bobbie Jean?" she asked. Nobody called me Bobbie Jean except people who have known me from elementary school days or Mama, when I was naughty.

"I'm ready," I replied.

Dale began the Wedding March. Before I realized it, I was saying "I do." Moments later, "You may kiss the bride" was spoken.

I'm Mrs. Bernard Jobe, I thought.

Anthony sat on Miss Turner's lap throughout the ceremony. She answered each question he asked. She stuffed him with cake and punch too.

The reception ended and people began drifting away. Mama said to Anthony, "Come on, Tony. Let's go."

"Come on, Mommie," he said to me.

"No, Tony, Bobbie is going with Bernard," Mama said.

"I'm going too," he insisted.

Mama said, "Not this time."

Anthony looked at us and back to Mama. "I knew I shouldn't let her marry him," came from my hurt son. Daddy left pulling him by one arm.

The next morning I opened my eyes. *No, it's not a dream.* The shiny gold band on my finger told me I really was married. The sleeping form beside me wore an identical wedding band.

A perfect day to begin married life, I thought while snuggling down to relish thoughts of our future. Outside snow quietly hit the window. Beautiful, white snow. Snow sent down for Mr. and Mrs. Bernard Jobe. *By the end of this week, we'll be moving to our home. I can't wait to live in our white cottage. God's giving us a home, just as we wanted.*

"Thank You, Father, for so much happiness. I never dreamed life could be so wonderful."

7

Nearly six weeks to the day after our wedding, the phone rang and I answered. Mama Daisy said,

"Bobbie, I think you need to come over here. Ruby Lee is sick."

"What's wrong with her?"

"She's hurting in her chest."

"Does she want to go to the Coffey Clinic?"

"I think so."

"Let me talk with her. Hello, Mama, what's wrong?"

"I've been sick all night, Bobbie. The hurting in my chest won't stop. I think I better go to the doctor. Your father didn't come home last night."

I called Miss Turner and told her I wouldn't be at work. Then I drove to Mama's house.

Mama lay in bed. "Oh, God!" I prayed for strength as I was really seeing Mama for the first time. No longer could I bury my head in the sand. Mama's condition was serious.

Dr. Bohl became Mama's doctor after Dr. Stow went into private practice. He entered the examination room and said to Mama, "I just finished looking at your X rays. I think I'm going to have a specialist check them too. I don't want to overlook anything. I'll let you know his decision."

He wrote a prescription to relieve pain and instructed her to rest and not worry. I drove her home and remained. She would not rest otherwise. *Where is my drunk father? If I could get my hands on him, I'd kill him. Doesn't he know how sick Mama is?* If thoughts could kill, Daddy would have died instantly.

It hurt to see Mama so sick. She refused to complain, though. While she dozed, I went into the bathroom. If she saw me cry she would know the seriousness of her condition,

"Father, please, Father, spare my mother. Don't let her die. I owe her too much. Let me make her life happy. Please God, save her."

Two days later, Mama received a call from Dr. Bohl. He wanted her to go to a cardiac specialist and had made the appointment.

"Bobbie, I hate to bother you. You and Jobe don't need my problems, but your father is no help right now. Will you go to the heart specialist with me?"

Nothing could have kept me from going with her. We waited together for her to be seen by Dr. McBride.

"Mrs. Ellis," the nurse called.

I helped Mama into the examination room. To see her smile, you wouldn't think she hurt. I knew differently. I recognized her grimaces of pain.

Dr. McBride studied Mama's latest chest X rays. He did an examination, paying special attention to the blood pressure, heart sounds, and the hint of any inadequate supply of oxygen in the blood.

"I think you need to have another test done. We probably can correct your problems, but I need the results of this test before we plan anything. Can you go to the hospital?"

"Yes, for how long?" Mama asked.

"I want to do a cardiac catheterization. You'll be back home after a couple of days."

"Will I need an operation?"

"Maybe. I'll know after the test.

"What will you do?"

"Doctor, I'll explain the test to her. I'm a registered nurse," I added.

"Good. I'll have my nurse reserve a bed for her at Saint Joseph. On the way out, check with her for instructions."

I helped Mama undress and get into bed as soon as we reached home. Mama Daisy came and sat in the chair beside the bed. She said nothing, but I knew she was worried. Usually, she would be piddling around the kitchen, singing about Jesus.

"Now, explain to me what he's going to do," Mama said.

"He's going to have you put to sleep, so he can work," I answered.

"Seriously, what does he plan to do?"

"He's going to put a very small catheter into a vessel of your arm and pass it up into your heart. The catheter can be seen by X ray, so he can tell things about your heart that don't show up on chest X rays."

"Is that all?"

"Scout's honor," I said.

"No cutting?" Mama asked.

"Just to place the catheter into the vessel. He'll tell you later about the surgery."

Mama settled back on her two fat pillows. They helped her breathe easier. I had satisfied her curiosity. She needed no worry of any type at this time. I could hear the "prodigal husband" preparing supper. Maybe he could resist drinking long enough to help Mama through this ordeal.

The night before the test was to be done, Nell and I entertained Mama. We acted like three college girls. Nobody wanted to think or talk about the next day.

"Well, Mama, visiting hours are over. I'll be here before they take you up, and I'll be here when you get back. Don't worry. Everything is going to be all right. This is no quack."

"I certainly hope not. And I'm hoping he has steady hands too. Do they ever have dumb doctors?"

"You better believe it!"

"He's not one, is he?"

"No, he has an excellent reputation." I kissed her and said, "See you tomorrow."

"Hi," Mama sleepily said, as her stretcher approached me the next morning.

I had waited at her bedside for her return. She was lifted onto the bed and the attendants left. She tried to talk but couldn't stay awake.

Dr. McBride entered. "Hi, Mrs. Jobe. Did she just get back?"

"Yes."

"Was she awake enough to talk?"

"No, not really."

"Come go to X ray with me. I'll show you her films."

While we walked, we talked. "My news is not very good. I was hoping to find an operable aneurysm. Your mother has three. I never saw a person with more than one. It's a miracle she lived this long. I can't believe she hasn't had more problems.

He located Mama's pictures and put them on the viewing screen. He pointed to one ballooning area on the ascending aorta and two on the descending aorta.

"Did you ever see an aneurysm this large?"

He outlined an unusually long ballooning area, covering a lengthy area of the descending aorta. He stood shaking his head, as if forgetting I were present.

"I can't operate. She would die on the table."

"What do we do?"

"Nothing. We keep her happy and comfortable as possible. I'll inform Dr. Bohl of my findings. He'll have to increase the pain medicine as the pain increases."

"How long does she have?"

"I'd say three to six months at the most."

"That's all?" I asked.

"She'll be doing well to live that long. Any one of these areas can rupture and kill her. It'll be like a blowout of a tire. Her condition is very grave."

I extended my hand for a farewell shake. "Thanks, Doctor."

I started back. My legs felt wobbly; my feet wore cement shoes. Once inside the public bathroom, I opened the flood gate of my tears. I don't know how long I remained there.

I have to go back; I can't. She needs me now more than ever; I can't tell her. Don't tell her. She'll know. No, she won't. Tell her she'll get the operation when Dr. McBride makes her stronger. My thoughts had rambled upon the answer. "Oh, God! Please, Father, don't take Mama. Don't take her. Go with me and help me keep her hope alive!"

I left the bathroom and started back to Mama. My legs became stronger and my feet accelerated. Jesus was at my side. I felt strength flowing to me, like hands carrying me. Mama was awake. I walked over and kissed her.

"I was afraid you weren't here," she said.

"I went with the doctor to see your X rays."

"When will he operate?"

"Don't rush," I said, smiling.

I had to prepare for the big lie. I looked at Mama. She waited to hear. I never learned to look directly at her while not telling the truth. Bluffing my way, I said, "Everything looks good, but he's going to have to build you up before he operates."

Mama said nothing. Her eyes penetrated my gaze. I lowered my eyes. She said, "I know. You don't have to pretend with me. I know I can't have the operation. How much longer do I have?"

I lost the bluff. I had nothing witty to say. Tears flowed silently down my face. Neither of us said anything. I sat holding her hand until Bernard came.

Mama was happy and kidding, as always, after Bernard's arrival. He sensed the news hadn't been good. He said nothing about test results. No one did.

As Dr. McBride said, Mama was home in a few days. Every day she had Daddy driving her somewhere. I couldn't catch up with her during the day. One evening, I called her,

"Where have you been?" I asked.

"Why aren't you at work?"

"I am at work. You're never home in the day anymore," I replied.

"There's too much to get done."

"Didn't Dr. McBride tell you to rest?"

"I don't have time to rest."

"What's so important you can't follow the doctor's orders?"

"I'm trying to take as much responsibility off you as possible."

"Like what, Mama?"

"I filed my will today, and I got my insurance beneficiaries corrected."

"Why are you doing all of that?"

"You know I don't have long."

"You're going to have your operat—"

She interrupted, "You can't tell me, but I know."

Again I lost the bluff.

Mama became top priority to Bernard and me. We talked with her each day and visited several times a week. I cooked dinner and invited them. We went shopping. Nothing could be delayed. Mama didn't have many tomorrows left.

"Bobbie, I want you to take Tony home with you and Jobe," Mama suggested during a visit.

"Why?" I asked in shock.

They loved Anthony and had begged to keep him a little longer after I married. I promised to let him stay an additional three months. The time would allow me to establish a relationship with Bernard. I never expected them to ask me to take him.

"I love him. Time's getting short for me. Your father will not do anything but spoil him. He needs to get to know Jobe."

Daddy chimed in, "I'll take care of him."

"You're not his father. He's got to know Jobe," Mama answered.

"Where he goes, I go," Daddy persisted.

Mama turned to me. "Baby, take your son with you, this evening. Your father is too unreliable to care for a five year old."

"I'll get my clothes too," Daddy said.

"Good," Mama said. "I bet Jobe sends you back."

The phone woke me a few days later. I answered.

"Your mother wants you to go to the doctor with her," Daddy reported.

"What's the matter?"

"She's hurting, and we haven't been able to stop the pain."

"I'll be there as soon as I dress." I drove to Mama's in prayer, "Please God, please. It hasn't been three months. It's only six weeks. Let her live. Please, God."

We sat in the examination room, waiting to hear Dr. Bohl's verdict.

"Ruby, you need extended care. I want to send you to the hospital in Marshall."

Terror filled Mama's eyes, then tears filled them. Dr. Bohl saw the reaction too. He continued, "You don't have to make a decision now. Let me know in a day or two. I'm going to have the nurse give you an injection to stop your pain and prescribe a stronger pill to control pain."

Mama had told me how she felt about the company hospital in Marshall, Texas. Three times she was successfully operated on there, but she believed she wouldn't be coming home if she went again.

On our way home, she asked, "What would you do?"

"I can't help you. It has to be your decision," I answered.

"I don't know what to do."

Mama dozed, while I prepared her lunch. She called to me, "Bobbie, will you come here?"

"Yes, what do you need?"

"Sit down. I hate to leave you, Baby, but I'm ready. Call Dr. Bohl and tell him to make the necessary arrangements."

"Are you sure, Mama?"

"I have no fear. I'm ready." She glanced at the Bible on the table beside her. "If I had it to do over, I wouldn't want to know."

"Mama, you knew!"

"I knew you couldn't tell me, so I asked Dr. Bohl."

"He told you?"

"Yes. I don't fear death. It's the waiting that's so hard." Tears filled her eyes. "Go ahead and call."

I made the call and reported back to Mama. "He'll call for an ambulance to come transport you to the hospital. He says, I have to escort you."

"You can't take off from work," she protested.

"I took off on Saturdays to find Bernard, didn't I?"

"But you don't know how long you'll be gone."

"Who cares? I don't have but one mother."

I went home to prepare my clothes after organizing Daddy and Mama Daisy. I called my job and informed them of the events taking place. Then I went back to help prepare Mama.

At four o'clock the ambulance from Marshall arrived. So did friends and neighbors. The house filled with those sending us off with their prayers.

Mama Daisy was her usual quiet self. I was seeing a different Mama Daisy too. She didn't cry at Grandpa's funeral, but a few tears slowly crept down her cheeks. I could see the bond between mother and child.

Daddy was quiet; Jean looked without understanding. Anthony ran from Mama to me crying, "Mommie, I want to go. Why, can't I go, Mommie? Nannie, take me."

Just before putting her on the stretcher, I gave Mama another pill to relieve the pain. I prayed she could sleep during the trip. This was a long journey for a person as critically ill as Mama.

I climbed in back with her. "Bye, bye," I called. Mama waved. Tears came when she waved to Jean and Anthony.

"Lord, can we make it in time?"

8

As I had hoped, Mama slept quietly. I started oxygen as soon as we began the trip. Each time she moved my heart jumped. I couldn't erase the thought of Mama's heart rupturing. How I would endure that moment, I wasn't sure. I wanted to support her, though, until the end.

Deep into East Texas, Mama totally woke up and began looking around.

"I think, I can do without the oxygen, Bobbie."

"Do you want to try?"

"Yes."

"You don't talk. Just listen. I'll talk for both of us," I said.

She smiled weakly. I said I would talk, but what do you talk about when your mother's dying?

"Mama, this is the highway we take to go to Bernard's home. He's from Hawkins, Texas. You'll have to look when I tell you to. If you don't, you'll miss seeing it."

Mama smiled.

"Yep, you can pass through downtown in one blink of your eyes."

"You're crazy," Mama chuckled.

Her smile was growing into a chuckle. The sound provoked more travelogue dialogue.

"Ladies and Gentlemen, turn left at the next intersecting road, and you'll find Aunt Mary's and Aunt Nita's houses."

"Who are they?"

"You're supposed to listen."

"I'm all right. I'll shut up if I get short winded."

"Aunt Mary and Nita are two women responsible for my husband. Bernard's mother died when he was fourteen. Along that road, you will discover the home Bernard Jobe lived in as a youngster. But you can't enter it."

"Why?"

"Because a sign in the front yard says, 'KEEP OUT'."

"It belongs to someone, else?"

"Yes and no. It's leased to an oil company. I married a man in oil. You didn't know that, did you?"

"No, and you didn't either, unless he's in cooking oil."

"I'm not kidding. In the front yard an oil well pump is in constant motion. It's not paying much these days, but it did in the past. There's a Jobe's cemetery too. Look Mama, that's Jarvis Christian College."

I talked; I didn't want to think. I had to keep Mama's spirits high. The ambulance driver must have known the serious condition of his passenger. He turned the emergency lights on to pass cars driving too slowly on the two-lane highway.

We arrived and Mama was put to bed. Oxygen was restarted. Orders had been left. She was given an injection because the pain worsened. Within minutes, she slept.

"Nurse, is there a hotel near here?" I inquired.

"Don't you intend to stay with her?"

"Yes."

"We made arrangements for you to stay in the room with her. You can take the other bed."

"Thank you."

"Thank you! We heard, you're a R.N. You can help with your mother's care. We have a nurse shortage here too."

Mama's condition slowly stabilized. I began to hope. As her strength increased, her independence did too. I opened my eyes early one morning and saw her in the bathroom.

"Mama, what are you doing out of bed?"

"I had to go to the bathroom."

"You're supposed to use this commode chair."

"I don't like that thing."

"You're not supposed to like it. You're supposed to use it."

"You have to empty it."

"So? What do you think, I'm here to do? Wake me next time."

Bathing her was a problem too. Each day our conversation sounded like an echo.

"Mama, I'm ready to give you your bath."

"I'll get up."

"No, you stay in bed. Your orders say you are to get a bed bath each day."

She cooperated only so long. "Put some soap on the towel, and I'll finish bathing," she'd ask.

"I'm supposed to bathe you, Mama."

"You are bathing me."

"I'm not through."

"You think you aren't. I can finish bathing myself."

Bernard and Anthony arrived for a visit Sunday evening. Daddy came Monday morning. I had been delighted to see my son and husband. Seeing Daddy produced anger. He hadn't come to help. He wanted to coerce Mama into changing her will.

Another week passed with no change in Mama's condition. I saw no need for both Daddy and me to remain. I began considering going home. It was apparent he didn't intend to leave.

"I talked with your doctor, and I'm thinking about going home. He says you can come, too, in a few days. I'll come back and ride back with you."

"All right," Mama replied without much emotion.

I thought, *All she has to say is she wants me to stay. I'll be glad to stay.*

"Mama, are you sure I can leave?"

"I'll be all right."

"Nell is across the hall. She'll call me if you need me."

"All right."

The evening I was to leave, I called a taxi and stood watching for its approach. Mama's window faced the highway.

"Mama, the bus will pass here. Look for me."

The bus was in the terminal when I arrived. I boarded and sat in a seat facing the direction of

Mama's room. As we neared the hospital, I pressed my face to the window. Mama didn't forget. Her drapes stood open, revealing the entire window. Mama sat in bed, looking out. We exchanged waves.

One week passed without any word. I considered no news as good news. She wasn't worse, at least. Thursday of the second week I talked with Mama and her doctor. She was ready to come home. At work, everyone saw my joy.

"Mrs. Jobe, I'm glad your mother is better."

"I'm going to bring her home tomorrow. The doctor says she's still critical but she can come if I ride back with her."

Bernard and I lay awake until the early morning hours, planning what we could do to increase Mama's happiness. I considered myself fortunate to have a husband who loved his mother-in-law.

Ring! Ring! Ring!

I jumped from bed and ran to the front door.

RING! It wasn't the door! It was the phone. I returned to the phone and answered it.

"I have a collect call for Bobbie Jobe from Tom Ellis. Will you accept the call?"

"Yes, Operator."

"Bobbie, she's gone. She just died. She's still in the room."

"No! No! I'm coming in a few hours."

"No, Baby, she's gone. Call Baker's and have them come pick her up. I'll ride back with them.

"Oh, my soul! No, my mother's not dead!"

Bernard took the receiver. Seconds later, I heard him trying to console me. "Baby, I'm here. I'm here."

I called Mama Daisy. She wasn't up yet. It was a few minutes after six o'clock. "Mama Daisy, Daddy called. Mama's dead."

"Oh my, this'll kill me," she moaned.

I could hear her crying; I heard Jean asking, "What's wrong, Mama Daisy?"

We joined Mama Daisy to share our grief. I pinched myself a few times. "It's real. My mother is dead." I had to hear myself say it aloud.

Daddy came, and we bombarded him with questions.

"Daddy, what happened?"

"I was sitting by her bed and she was sitting up. She coughed, and a little blood came up. She coughed a few seconds later, and more blood came up. She coughed the third time, and a lot of blood came up. She put her hand over her heart and just said, 'Well, that did it.' "

"That did what?" I asked.

"She said, 'That's all of it. Call the nurse.' She made three snoring sounds and was gone before the nurses came. They put oxygen on her, but it was no use."

Mama had tried repeatedly to discuss what was to be done when she died; I stopped her each time. I saw the X rays, but believed God would intervene.

"I guess we'll go to Baker's and start making the arrangements," I suggested.

"I think your mother has all ready done that," Daddy said.

"When?"

"I took her one day we were out. She wanted to go."

"I'll call and ask," I insisted. I made the call and returned to Daddy. "You're right. Mama picked the casket and completed nearly all the arrangements. We need to select the family flowers and her shroud."

We began the tremendous task of contacting family members and friends. The response we received would determine Mama's funeral date.

"Daddy, so far people are coming from Saint Louis, Phoenix, Los Angeles, Kansas City, and all over the state of Texas. I had no idea, so many people knew Mama."

"Your mother had many friends," Daddy said.

The day before the funeral, Mama was brought home as she had requested. People came and went all day. That night our six-room house bulged with people. The crowd had little in common except their love of Mama.

Each room took on a characteristic. Church friends and elderly people occupied one room, neighbors and co-workers another, my professional associates, whites, and young adults shared another; Daddy's drinking friends another; Jean and children her age were in another; and anyone needing to rest found peace and seclusion in the last room.

I wandered from room to room, talking with the occupants. My nerves were frayed. Daddy waited, until this day, to start drinking. He wanted to wander and talk too.

Bernard pulled me into the kitchen and said, "Bobbie, why don't you leave Tom alone? You're upsetting yourself."

"I don't want anyone to know he's been drinking."

"If they know him, they know he drinks."

Daddy's voice bellowed from another room. I tried to contain him all night.

Around five the morning of the funeral, I started to the bathroom and caught a glimpse of Daddy. He sat at Mama's head with his head lowered. Tears dripped onto his chest.

Daddy loves Mama. I can understand his drinking. He doesn't want to think of living without her. Thirty-two years of married life can't be replaced very soon.

A week passed before I began putting Mama's clothes away. The new clothes we bought on a shopping trip remained new. Price tags hadn't been removed. A cedar chest was filled with new linens, and the kitchen contained dishes and silver used for special occasions. Grief overpowered me about halfway through the ordeal.

"I want my Mama," I cried. I couldn't stop. I was upsetting Mama Daisy, so I hurried to the bathroom. "Father, I hurt so badly. Why did You take my mama? I wanted to make her happy."

Each time, I questioned why Mama died, I became thankful, too. "Father, I thank You for not letting Mama suffer or linger. She could have had a stroke and lay in bed for years, but You gave her rest. Thank You, Father."

Mama was the hub of the entire household. Without her, the family unit fell apart. Mama made me promise I would give Jean back to her mother. Bennie Ruth flew from Los Angeles and took Jean back.

Mama Daisy was at a loss. She had loved and cared for Jean since she was two months old. She didn't know how to live without her. I searched daily for someone to stay with her. She wasn't senile or incapacitated, but she needed companionship.

People promised to help and didn't. Mama Daisy supplied the answer. "I talked with Jesus. He's coming to get me. I'm going to live with them."

Daddy wasn't my concern. He drank daily. Once drunk, he'd call and verbally abuse me. He tried to obtain the family car and some real estate and discovered he couldn't.

Mama had said, "I'm leaving everything to you, Bobbie. Your daddy will drink and squander it if I leave it to him. I ask you to let him live in the home place as long as he wants."

The homestead stood vacant after Mama Daisy left. Daddy chose to move to the surroundings of his drinking pals. He didn't let up on the verbal attacks, though.

One evening, Bernard was home during an encounter. I hung up, shaking and in tears. He counseled, "Why do you talk to him while he's drinking? He's not responsible now. Hang up when you hear his voice." The next day, I took my husband's advice.

Except for Bernard, my life contained little joy. Things worsened at work. I worked as evening charge nurse on the Hospital Ward; I really wanted to work with the team treating mental problems.

A Friday evening, I received a call from Mrs. Oustaian. "Mrs. Jobe (she pronounced it Jo Be), you will report to the operating room Monday morning. Fannie needs a scrub nurse."

The weekend was miserable. I counted the advantages of the new position. I would have every weekend off, would work only days, would begin each day at 8 instead of 6:45, and would be in an air conditioned-environment. Everything I wanted!

No, I hated thinking about the new assignment. It was another step away from my desires. How could I talk with anesthetized patients?

As I unlocked my door one night, the phone began to ring. "Hang on! Hang on, I'm coming." I fumbled with the key. Finding the keyhole in the dark wasn't easy.

Ring!

"Whoever it is doesn't intend to hang up." I ran, picked up the receiver, and heard,

"I have a collect call for Bobbie Jobe from Jessie Baldwin. Will you accept the call?"

"Yes, Operator." My legs were jelly.

"Your grandmother has had a stroke. She was in the hospital a week. She went to a nursing home today. I thought you should know."

"I'll be there in the morning, Uncle Jessie."

We left for Houston at six the next morning. I couldn't verbalize my fears. I rode and prayed silently: "Please Father, let me do for Mama Daisy the things I wanted to do for Mama."

Uncle went with us to the nursing home and straight to Mama Daisy's room. Seeing her brought a tightness around my chest. The stroke had been a major one.

She was totally paralyzed on the left side and couldn't speak. Her skin was hot and very dry, and her heels were puffy. Her skin would start breaking down soon.

I was aware of her watching my expression while I examined her. My mind tried to form a plan. I didn't want to leave her in Houston, and I couldn't care for her at home. She saw Anthony and started trying to talk to him. I was free to discuss the situation with Bernard.

"Mama Daisy, I want to carry you home. Do you understand?"

She gave a weak nod for yes.

"Do you want to go back to Fort Worth?"

She repeated the affirmative nod.

"I can't take care of you at home. I'll have to put you in a home, but I'll be close enough to come everyday. Is that all right with you?"

She nodded yes.

"We're going home this evening. I'll arrange for an ambulance to pick you up Monday morning. Do you understand?"

Yes she nodded.

My nursing instincts took charge. I sponged her and gave her oral hygiene, massaged the areas most likely to form bed sores, and started her drinking fluids.

"We have to go. Remember, I'm sending for you Monday morning." I kissed her good-bye after saying, "I love you."

Our return trip to Fort Worth was swift. Arrangements had to be started before the work day ended. Nothing could be done on Saturday or Sunday.

"I found a home for her, Bernard. It's a nice place. They give good nursing care."

Sunday night I arrived from church as the phone rang. My heart pounded. *Please God, don't let it be bad news.* "Hello."

"I have a collect call for Bobbie Jobe from Jessie Baldwin. Will you accept the call?"

I managed to say "Yes."

"Bobbie, we've been trying to get you all evening," Aunt Alma reported. "Honey, your grandmother died this evening."

I hung up and sat waiting for Bernard to come. I didn't cry; I felt as though no tears remained.

Baker's hearse made the trip to bring Mama Daisy home. I wasn't spared making her final arrangements. All decisions were mine to make. Mama was buried March thirty-first and Mama Daisy August eighth. Same church and same minister.

Bernard saw I wasn't coping with the situation as I should. When Uncle Jessie arrived from Houston, Bernard said, "Let's drive your uncle home after the funeral. We can go to Galveston a few days."

I agreed. I didn't care whether or not I went. I was dead inside.

Bernard continued, "I'll call Louise and Leldon. They'll go with us."

I had met Bernard's cousin a few weeks previously. Maybe, they could help me feel alive again.

Life became a treadmill of joyless days after returning to Fort Worth. I walked, talked, worked, and ate out of habit. Inside, I remained dead. "Bernard, I'm so tired. I feel like I haven't slept at all," I said as I climbed from bed.

"Maybe you need some vitamins."

"I need something. I'm nearly too tired to walk."

We were watching TV the next week when Bernard asked, "Does your chest ever hurt?"

"No, why?"

"As much as you cough, it has to hurt."

"It doesn't, though."

I had noticed the frequency and severity of my cough but had said nothing. It concerned me. No mucus was ever produced, but I couldn't control it. *Tuberculosis* began floating in and out of my thoughts.

Washing my face a few days later, I realized the lymph nodes of my face and neck were greatly enlarged. I could feel a large one on the left side of my face. None were painful. *I must have an infection somewhere,* I reasoned.

Miss Harrison was able to release me from the operating room after a new staff nurse was hired. I was glad to return to the infirmary ward.

I had been accused of giving special attention to certain addicts when it wasn't true. I opened the grill door one afternoon to a new admission who would occupy many hours of my thoughts.

"Hello, I'm Mrs. Jobe."

"I'm Sanchez," he stated in a noncaring manner.

I was assembling his chart, when my eyes fell on his symptoms: constantly tired, slight nausea, enlarged lymph nodes, frequent cough. The similarity of our symptoms stunned me. I thumbed through the forms, looking for a diagnosis.

Hodgkin's disease occupied that spot. Other patients ill with Hodgkins died or became critical. *I can't have this disease*, I thought within my brain.

As days became weeks, everyone realized Sanchez was dying. He knew it too. His adjustment was not acceptance. He became irritable and cursed the staff at the slightest provocation. I talked with him in spite of his verbal rejection. My symptoms hadn't disappeared; if anything, my nodes were larger. I questioned Dr. Grimm about Hodgkin's, trying to find some way to rule it out in my case. I hadn't been able to voice my fears to anyone.

Sanchez lowered his guard after I refused to stay away from him. "Jobe, I know I'm dying. Why don't they let me go home to die?"

"They are trying to release you. But federal prisoners can't go without permission."

"This is something. Twenty-five years old and dying." He shook his head as if in disbelief. I didn't know how to answer him. A beautiful baby's picture sat on his bedside table.

"That's a beautiful baby," I said to change the subject.

"She has to be. I'm her daddy," he proudly answered.

"Where is she?"

"She lives with my mother."

"You aren't married?"

"Yeah, my old lady got busted for the same drug

case I did. She's doing time in Lexington. Jobe, I want to see my daughter one more time before I die. I'm praying I can go home."

One day, Sanchez was positive. Next day, he was negative. "Jobe, tell these people to let me go. You know what I'd do?

"No, I don't."

"I'm dying, right? I'd find a way to kill myself."

I listened more than I talked. I didn't know how to answer him. I couldn't encourage him when new symptoms developed daily.

Sanchez's abdominal lymph nodes became large prior to receiving permission for a transfer. He wasn't going home. He was being sent to a prison hospital. A few weeks after Sanchez left, we received word that he had gone blind. Someone wrote the letter for him. I cried because my future was uncertain too.

I'll tell Bernard tonight.

"Call and make an appointment to see Dr. Bohl," Bernard said after I told him.

"All right," I answered.

"If you don't go, I'll take you," he came back.

"I'll call."

I went to the doctor the next day. I related each symptom and the length of their presence to Dr. Bohl. He followed up with a thorough physical.

"Can you go to the hospital?

"Yes, but I don't want to."

"You have no choice. I need to biopsy one of those nodes. They should not stay enlarged, like this. How soon can you go?"

"Whenever you say."

He returned, shortly. "I have arranged for you to enter Doctor's General tomorrow."

The node on the side of my face was removed. I woke and felt the bandage covering the area. "They shaved my hair!"

Nausea nearly brought vomiting, but wanting to see my head forced it back. Any nurse knows the operative area has to be shaved. *I should have told him to get another node,* I thought, while looking into the mirror. Just the edge of the hairline had been shaved. It would grow back, I hoped.

"You can forget Hodgkins. Your biopsy was negative."

"You're sure. You wouldn't withhold information, would you?" I asked.

"Here, read your chart."

I read until I was satisfied. Hodgkins wasn't on any of the reports.

"Your results are positive for Boeck's Sarcoidosis, though."

I had not heard of the condition; I waited for Dr. Bohl to continue. "No one knows what causes it, so there's no cure. It usually doesn't cause any problems. If problems develop, they're in the lungs most of the time. But it can attack any system. I need to do more tests to be sure you're all right. I'm ordering an X ray of your hands and chest, an EKG, and some special eye examinations.

Each test result read, *Negative.*

I returned to work. Physically I felt fine. My symptoms disappeared. Dr. Bohl was correct. Sarcoid and

I could live together. Life had to have more meaning, though. I resigned my position three years and one day after being hired. Off I went in search of new friends and nursing adventures.

Mrs. Hazlewood, another R.N., encouraged me to seek employment at a local hospital. "I know the director of nursing. I'll give you a reference. You'll like working there. They are progressive and have some of the latest equipment," she counseled.

After two weeks of rest, I inquired about a position with the hospital Mrs. Hazlewood had recommended.

Monday morning the following week I sat in Personnel. No one talked about overthrowing the government or contraband substances. I didn't remain half a day in Personnel, either. I stayed the entire day with the director of Inservice.

"Mrs. Jobe, report to Nursing Service, each morning. Mrs. Appleman will orient you to hospital rules and regulations. She will also demonstrate the latest equipment being used. You'll find nursing the private patient is quite different from your past experiences."

Louise Appleman was responsible for my orientation. She couldn't have been much older than I, if she were as old, but she was director of Inservice already. Most head nurses were our age. Advancements were given on merit, not seniority.

I could hardly wait to make new friends. I would have plenty of them too. I wasn't working on a unit, but everyone seemed in a hurry to meet me. Each day people welcomed me to the hospital.

Louise accompanied me to lunch daily. I'd be her shadow for two weeks before being turned loose.

"Bobbie, have you noticed, you haven't seen any other black nurses?" Louise asked.

"Yes, I have. I intended to ask you about that."

"We don't have any more."

"On this shift?" I questioned.

"No, employed by the hospital."

"Registered Nurses?"

"We don't have any black nurses."

"On this shift?" I questioned.

"No, you're the only one employed by this hospital."

"Do you mean, Nursing Service has no blacks?"

"You're the only one. Does that bother you?"

"I guess not, now that I'm here."

It had taken them four days to tell me. I wondered if Mrs. Hazlewood had known I would be the only black nurse. Blacks filled housekeeping, dietary, the laundry, and transported patients between X ray and physical therapy. Louise's comments shed light on the conversations I had with other blacks. Each one spoke nearly identical words. "Welcome to the hospital. How do you like it here? Do they treat you all right?" Everyone except me knew I was the only black nurse in the hospital. I couldn't wait to tell Bernard the news. That night I repeated my conversation with Louise.

Bernard remarked, "Baby, you must feel like you're the only fly in the buttermilk."

"I certainly can't hide! I understand, too, why the director of Nursing said I would be assigned to night duty to allow people to become accustomed to my presence."

"How do you think you're going to like it?"

"I don't have a problem with people. Your wife can relate to anyone."

Instead of receiving a ward assignment, I reported to Nursing Service each night. From there, I was dispatched to any floor not staffed with a registered nurse.

"How are you liking your job?" Bernard asked after a month passed.

"I love it. I'm getting to do the good nursing care I was taught to do. I'm not afraid someone will say I'm being seductive."

Life is filled with contradictions. I was happy; I was sad too. I worked with a competent crew who valued my opinions and followed my instructions. We lost one or two patients a week. Cancer defeated our best efforts.

"Nurse, can I get well? Can I be healed? I hurt so much. Oh, please, don't let me wake up in the morning! Nurse, give me something to end this torture. Nurse, can I be healed?" The little lady had cancer of the bones. Someone fractured a collar bone while moving her about. Four of us worked together when we did anything for her. She didn't weigh a hundred pounds, but no one wanted to risk breaking a bone. No one attempted to answer her ramblings. We didn't have answers and didn't want to instill false hope.

Preparing the nurse's report, I realized more than half the patients had some type of cancer and were dying. We calculated the average age and couldn't believe our findings. It was twenty-five years old!

I made rounds twice nightly to check each patient and provided or directed the care of those critical and dying.

Walking from the parking lot one night, tears and words poured out. "Oh, God! I need Your help! I don't know what to say to my patients. How can I encourage them? Father, forgive me for not talking with You since Mama Daisy's death. Forgive me for blaming You. Show me how to extend hope."

My duties were light that night. Most had cancer and one died, but peace and calmness replaced sadness and distress. God added four "work tools" to augment my skills: empathy, to guide my decisions and actions; ears to listen for the unspoken; prayer to bring help from heaven; and a sincere touch to send forth the message of understanding and concern.

"You must be Mrs. Jobe," a middle-aged white lady said, as I started rounds one night.

"Yes, I am."

"My husband talks about you all the time." She realized I didn't know who she was or who her husband was. She continued, "I'm Mrs. Wommack, George Wommack's wife."

"Yes, I remember Mr. Wommack. Is he still in Intensive Care?"

"No, he's on this floor."

"I didn't know that. I'm usually in Intensive Care myself."

"I was hoping to get to meet you. I wanted to thank you for everything you've done for George."

"It was my pleasure."

"He's cranky; he's not like that most of the time," the wife continued.

"I understand."

Mr. Wommack was dying from cancer of the lungs —fifty-one years old and diagnosed less than six months. He had been my only patient during the first days of his admission. I had stayed busy keeping his chemotherapy on schedule, doing hourly routines, maintaining I.V. flows, or changing his linens.

Perspiration had dripped from Mr. Wommack's body. I had changed his bed three or four times some shifts. We had talked when he couldn't sleep.

"Jobe, this is tough. I can't smoke without coughing like I'm dying."

"Oh, dear Lord! Oh, please! Help me!"

I sat behind the desk preparing the nightly reports. Loud screaming at 3 AM startles anyone. I started running down the darkened hall toward the screams; Mrs. Wommack was running toward me.

"Help me, somebody," she screamed. We passed each other without a word exchanged. I ran into Mr. Wommack's room and nearly fainted!

He sat on the side of his bed. Blood gushed, in one continuous stream, from his nose and mouth. He was trying to catch it in a trash can.

"Lord, help him!" I screamed, as I took a position of support in front of him. I felt the weight of his body growing heavier in my hands. I looked at his fingernails. A dusty blue hue replaced the usual pinkness.

"He's dying! God, help him!"

I looked at the call bell but couldn't reach it, unless

I turned Mr. Wommack loose. I couldn't turn him loose because I was his only support. I was having difficulty keeping him from falling to the floor. I eased him back on his pillow. Mr. Wommack was no longer with us.

I returned to the desk and attempted to answer the questions of my staff. Seeing their blood soaked-nurse nearly brought a panic.

I went to the lounge to clean up. Outside the lounge I heard my confused staff. Serenity surrounded me. "Father, I thank You for being with me through that ordeal. I could not have endured without You. I pray You will guide me in all my nursing duties."

When I told Bernard and Anthony of Mr. Wommack's death, Anthony's reaction revealed his maturity. He questioned, "Why do people have to die? Mommie, why can't they find a cure for cancer? Maybe, I'll find a cure when I grow up," he added, as tears rolled down his cheeks.

"Bernard, you should stop smoking," I urged.

"Why?"

"If you could have seen Mr. Wommack, you wouldn't ask why you should stop."

"People who haven't smoked a day in their life die from lung cancer too. What about them?"

"No one has the answer, but Mr. Wommack said that he wished he never had started. He coughed nearly thirty minutes after one inhale."

"You have to die from something, Bobbie."

"True, but there can be an easier way than hemorrhaging to death."

"Dying is dying," was his answer.

"Just thought I would warn you," I said.

"Thank you."

I ended the conversation. Bernard's sarcastic tone told me he wasn't ready to quit smoking.

The night after Mr. Wommack's death, I went to work and discovered that I was sort of a celebrity. The hospital buzzed about my performance. Mr. Wommack's roommate had praised my actions. Instead of waiting in the hall, as I had instructed, he watched from the door.

"Yea! Yea! We get Mrs. Jobe, tonight," an LVN said when I entered the nurses' station. "We like to work with you. You don't mind working."

"All registered nurses work," I replied.

"You ought to be ashamed for saying that. Your relief wouldn't come from behind this desk unless the hospital was on fire!"

I felt good being accepted and liked, especially since my entire crew was white. I remained "a fly in the buttermilk."

A few weeks later, I prepared to make my rounds.

"Mrs. Jobe, I'll check these rooms," an aide volunteered.

She handed me a slip of paper containing about six room numbers. "You don't need to go in their rooms. I'll tell you if they need something."

I heard her, but my brain wasn't assimilating her statements. The aide saw my confusion and continued, "Mrs. Brown will be up in a minute to talk to you." She walked away in a flash.

Something's up, and I'm the only one in the dark,

I thought. *My co-workers are avoiding my questions. Why does the supervisor need to talk with me? I can't recall doing anything wrong.*

"Mrs. Jobe, can I speak with you a minute?" Mrs. Brown asked.

I followed her to the lounge.

"Mrs. Jobe, you're an excellent nurse, and we consider ourselves fortunate to have you. You have done nothing wrong, but I was told to tell you, Dr. _____ and Dr. _____ went to Nursing Service today and complained. They requested that no black nurses care for their patients. They don't want you to enter the rooms or write on the charts."

"How am I supposed to care for their patients if I can't enter the rooms and I'm the only RN on duty?"

"Your aides and LVN will tell you of any problems, and you tell them what to do. If it's something a RN has to do, page one of the nursing supervisors. We'll come and do it."

"Did the patients complain?"

"No, just the doctors. I don't understand it. When they get to know you, they'll change their minds."

"I'll have fewer patients to worry about," I snapped.

"I'm sorry. Nursing Service doesn't agree with them, but doctors have the right to say what they want and don't want done to their patients."

She left and I remained in the lounge. I had blurted out a witty remark as if I weren't hurt. How could I finish the night?

I returned to the floor. All eyes searched my face

for a hint of my reaction to the news. Slowly and cautiously the subject was approached.

"Mrs. Jobe, we love you. You're a darn good nurse. We couldn't believe Dr. _____ and Dr. _____ would do such a thing. Remember, we enjoy working with you."

Bernard prepared for work as I undressed to go to bed. "What's wrong? You're too quiet," he said.

His simple remark brought the tears I had fought to hold back.

"Baby, what's wrong? Stop crying and tell me what's wrong. If you don't stop crying, I'll be late for work."

Finally, I repeated the conversation.

"What did you say when she told you what they said?"

"What could I say?"

"You were supposed to quit. You are quitting, aren't you?"

"I don't know."

"I can't believe you, Bobbie Jean. You don't have to take that kind of treatment; I don't expect you to. I want you to quit. Do you hear?"

I nodded yes.

"Call in and tell them you won't be back."

"Let me find another job first. A bird in the hand is better than two in the bush." I began job hunting that week.

One night I arrived on the floor and was instructed to call Mrs. Brown.

"Dr. _____ has had a severe stroke. He's in Intensive Care. He's unconscious and may not make it. He needs a good R.N. tonight. Will you consider special-ing him?"

"Didn't you say he may not make it?"

"Yes, he's critical."

"You want me to special him?"

"He needs the best tonight."

"I can't special him. Two weeks ago he said I wasn't to enter his patient's rooms. Have you forgot-ten?"

"He won't know. He's unconscious."

"I'll give him my best," I said. "I'll take care of him as much as I can."

"If you need me for anything, let me know," Mrs. Brown answered.

With four years nursing experience under my cap, I felt I didn't have to take the first job available. I wanted to work days and have weekends off.

Someone asked if I thought of Visiting Nursing. The question took roots. I tracked down each rumor and fact. I received a passing grade on the Merit Examination for Public Health Nurse I and was hired.

Knowing I had another position gave me boldness. I told a co-worker, "They can't do anything but fire me. I have my letter of resignation, so I don't care. I'm not going to nurse long distance anymore. I'll be taking care of all the patients on this floor."

My last night to work, the other doctor who didn't want me to enter his patient's rooms came at around 6 AM to check his patients. Everyone looked tense. I was charting on one of the forbidden charts. An aide gathered his charts, while I continued writing.

"I need Mrs. Johnson's chart. It's not here," the doctor announced.

"I have it," I replied. My steady gaze told him that I knew what he said to the director of nurses and what I thought of his comments.

"I'm in no hurry. You can finish charting," he answered.

He sat telling jokes, while I deliberately delayed giving him the chart. Everyone laughed except me. My actions spoke loudly.

The shift ended, and I went to Nursing Service as requested.

"Mrs. Jobe, you have been an excellent nurse. We hate to lose you. We're opening a Cardiac Care Unit next week. I would love to make you Assistant Head Nurse on that unit if you will stay with us. It's a day job with every third weekend off."

"It sounds good, but I begin work Monday as a Public Health Nurse."

"I hate to lose you. Come back and work part-time if you ever need extra money."

I located my time card and placed it in the time clock. As it printed my departure time, I realized another door of life was closing. God had already opened the door for my next entrance.

"I'm ready, Lord. Let's go!"

Epilogue

The Lord has led me through many doors since I left the hospital to be a Public Health Nurse. At every turn, I have felt the Lord's loving care. In fact, the disease I considered my enemy—Boeck's Sarcoidosis —put me in closer touch with Jesus.

I had been ill for three months and couldn't even remember simple instructions. I was unable to walk unassisted and any attempt to stand caused projectile vomiting. My neurosurgeon told me six conditions could cause these symptoms. He prescribed the steroid Decadron. It was my "miracle drug." After one day of medication, my symptoms disappeared. I was overjoyed!

Though my doctor had said, "You probably will never have this problem again," he didn't share my joy over the relief the medicine gave me. He said, "If your head ever hurts like that again, come back to me at once."

The following June I realized my head was pounding daily, and the world was growing darker. I was going blind! While in the hospital fighting my way through that crisis, I began to think that my son Anthony needed to know Jesus. I left the hospital with plans to help him begin a permanent walk with Christ.

The next year, I returned to the hospital one day before we were to depart on a vacation to California. I was crushed and so tired of being sick, but five holes had been discovered in my lungs.

It took three months to fight my way back—three months of rest. I learned to remain quiet by reading. Helen Steiner Rice became my daily friend. She knew Jesus! I mean really knew Him. When I read her poetry, I stood with Jesus just as she did.

My entire life was changing. I did not enjoy the things I once did. My taste in music even changed. I wanted to know the same Jesus Mrs. Rice knew.

The sicker I became, the more I fell in love with life. I began to look at the world differently; it was filled with beauty! The Bible also became understandable to me for the first time.

The following year I entered the hospital again. My brain was being attacked once more. When Bernard and Anthony went home after I was settled in my room, I got on my knees and talked with my Father.

"Father, I don't know what's wrong within my brain, but I ask You to show Dr. Webster the problem and reveal to him what to do about it."

Twenty-one days later, I heard Dr. Webster calling me from my anesthetized sleep. "I know what your problem is now, Mrs. Jobe," he said. He had drilled a hole into my skull, so he could look at my brain.

"Is there anything you can do for it?" I questioned.

"Yes, we'll go to surgery in a day or two. You rest now."

I was very sleepy, but I remembered my prayer on admission night. "Thank You, Jesus" came from my lips as joy warmed my heart.

The day Dr. Webster did the surgery I had no fear. I knew the same Jesus Mrs. Rice wrote of. If I lived or died I would always walk with Him. My reading for that day was entitled, "Where you are now, so is God." It seemed to be written just for me.

One year later I fought my last battle with Sarcoidosis. I was dying. My brain could not take steroids another day, but my lungs needed them daily or they would hemorrhage.

Standing in my kitchen one morning, trying to decide to take the pills or not take them, I heard myself say in a loud voice, "Jesus! Today You will heal me or I will die. I will not live like this another day, and I'm not going to take another pill!"

I couldn't believe I had spoken those words. But I decided to remain firm about them.

Today I am in perfect health. I have no holes in my lungs, and I have not required any additional steroids. God has a total plan for your life and mine. I'm allowing Him to reveal my reason for living. He opens doors for me that I never imagined entering.

For the past six months I have entered the federal prison to teach a parenting class.

Most of the students are college graduates and professionals. As I speak about Christ in my life, they hang onto each word. I see them sitting on the edge of their chairs. They hunger to know Christ as I did when I read Mrs. Rice's poem, "God, Are You There?"

After each class someone waits and asks me to pray about a problem in their life.

God does open the doors, and I thank Him for preparing me to follow Him through them. I desire to be in His tracks for all eternity.

You can, too. He's waiting to hear you call, "Father." Do it now. The door stands open.